T&

HANDMADE
MARKETPLACE

KARI CHAPIN

Illustrated by Emily Martin (a.k.a. The Black Apple) and Jen Skelley

Storey Publishing

dedication

To my amazing husband, Eric,
without whom this book never, ever would have happened.
Thank you, Eric, for everything.

The mission of Storey Publishing is to serve our customers by
publishing practical information that encourages
personal independence in harmony with the environment.

Edited by Deborah Balmuth and Dale Evva Gelfand
Art direction and book design by Alethea Morrison
Text production by Jennifer Jepson Smith

Cover and part opener illustrations by © Emily Martin
Spot illustrations by © Jen Skelley
Border and frame illustrations by Alethea Morrison

Indexed by Mary McClintock

Storey Publishing
210 MASS MoCA Way
North Adams, MA 01247
www.storey.com

Printed in the United States by Versa Press
10 9 8 7 6 5 4 3 2 1

Library of Congress Cataloging-in-Publication Data

Chapin, Kari.
  The handmade marketplace / Kari Chapin.
    p. cm.
  Includes index.
  ISBN 978-1-60342-477-6 (pbk. : alk. paper)
  1. Handicraft industries. 2. Selling—Handicraft. I. Title.
HD9999.H362C53 2010
745.5068'8—dc22
                                        2009049212

acknowledgments

Thank you to everyone at Storey Publishing: Deborah Balmuth, who helped me refine my idea and gave me this chance; Amy Greeman, who makes me laugh and treats me to sushi when I need it; Alethea Morrison, who has to be the most talented art director in all the land and she always makes time to answer my many questions; and Dale Evva Gelfand, for being amazing at what she does.

Thank you Emily Martin and Jen Skelley for your enchanting illustrations.

To my family: Ron and Robyn Chapin and Janis McWayne, the best parents a girl could ever hope for; Euretta Chapin, my wonderfully talented and creative sister; and Sharon Jandrow, who is the exact opposite of what I thought a mother-in-law would be like. Thank you for always believing in me and for your unending encouragement. I'm a lucky girl to have all of you.

To my urban family, the girls who made me who I am: Karolyn Tregembo, Sheila Weisenborn Borderick, and Kyme Vincent.

Thank you from the bottom of my crafty heart to the very best friends a girl could ever have: Karie Sutherland, Amanda Struse, Lisa Holman, and Minna Wallace.

I would also like to extend a special thank you to my creative life coach, Cynthia Gunsinger (www.gunsinger.com). Her expert guidance and incredible ability to help me sort out my thoughts have been invaluable to me, not only while writing this book, but in defining my goals in general. Cynthia, you are a superhero to me.

This book exists in part because of NPR, *Buffy the Vampire Slayer*, *Project Runway*, Neko Case, and Squam Art Workshops.

My heart swells when I think of my online craft community, including you, my readers. The inspiration I get from the members of my Creative Collective, online marketplaces, craft fairs, blogs, and podcasts makes me fantastically happy and fills my whole world with possibility and light. I am forever grateful for the connections and friendships that have formed out of our shared love for all things handmade.

Lastly, I am so thankful for my husband, Eric Nixon, and our little family: Baxter, Charlie Parker, and Zoe.

CONTENTS

Introduction, 1
My Creative Collective, 4

Part 1

Getting to Know Yourself and Your Business

CHAPTER 1: SETTING THE SCENE FOR SUCCESS *12*

Setting Goals * Build a Nurturing Space * Getting Unstuck *
Translating an Idea into Reality

CHAPTER 2: BRANDING YOUR BUSINESS *27*

Who Are Your Customers? * What's Your Message and Look? *
What's in a Name? * Develop a Logo

CHAPTER 3: ESTABLISHING BASIC BUSINESS PRACTICES *37*

What Kind of Business Are You? * The Next Steps *
Collecting Money * Pricing Your Work * Hiring Help

Part 2

Spreading the Word — and Images

CHAPTER 4: MARKETING BASICS *64*

Marketing Defined * Essential Marketing Materials *
Photographs Are Key

CHAPTER 5: YOUR CRAFT COMMUNITY *76*

Making Connections * Online Communities * Community Swaps

CHAPTER 6: BLOGGING *84*

Blogs and Websites Defined * Basic Setup * Writing a Successful Blog *
Give and Take * What Makes a Blog Successful * Create an Online Newsletter

CHAPTER 7: ADVERTISING AND PUBLICITY *107*

Advertising Online * Be Your Own Best Ad Agency *
Attracting Media Attention * Approaching Print Media *
Putting Together a Press Kit * Writing Press Releases

CHAPTER 8: MORE ONLINE MARKETING NETWORKS *128*

Podcasting * Social Media

Part 3

Getting Down to Selling

CHAPTER 9: **THE CRAFT FAIR SCENE** *146*

First Things to Know * The Fair Application Process * Getting the Word *
Preparing for the Fair * Designing Your Booth Space * Fair Day Etiquette *
Starting Your Own Craft Fair

CHAPTER 10: **SELLING IN ONLINE STORES** *171*

Evaluating Marketplaces * Setting Up Your Online Shop *
Customer Service * Answering Customer Questions and Comments

CHAPTER 11: **SELLING IN BRICK-AND-MORTAR STORES** *191*

Getting Your Foot in the Door * Persuasive Leave-Behind Materials *
Meeting with the Store Owner/Manager * Selling on Consignment

CHAPTER 12: **GET CREATIVE: OTHER SELLING OPTIONS
AND OPPORTUNITIES** *202*

Join a Co-Op * Teach a Course * Hold Trunk Shows *
Host House Parties * Offer Kits and Patterns

Parting Advice, 208
Resources, 211
Craft Show Supplies Checklist, 214
Index, 215

INTRODUCTION

Why do you craft? Are you compelled to create something with your hands? Are you looking for ways to save money or reuse what would normally be wasted? Maybe you grew up in a home that valued creating things together, and you just never stopped making stuff. Maybe it's like therapy for you, or you enjoy designing, or maybe you just dig the process more than the end result.

When I began writing this book, I asked my mother what her earliest memories of me crafting were. She told me how when I was around four years old, someone gave her nail polish she was discarding, and Mom and I used it like paint on salt-dough ornaments for our holiday tree. (I still have a small salt-dough heart ornament inscribed with my name; it is one of my greatest treasures.) As I grew up, I remember lots of crafting around the house: making playhouses out of washing machine boxes with my father, watching my stepmother sew quilts for me and my sister, and creating numerous collages and paper chains with my mom. When I was in the fourth grade, I learned to crochet. Since then I've been, well, hooked on crafting.

Crafting relaxes me and helps me de-stress. When I'm working on a project, I feel peaceful and calm; my hands seem to have a mind of their own, and my brain relaxes. Some people do their best thinking in the shower or while driving; for me, my best thinking happens when I'm up to my elbows in vintage buttons or cutting out inspiring images from magazines or winding yarn.

I also find crafting a release. It makes me feel useful and whole. An activity as simple as sewing a button back onto my husband's winter coat brings me much more personal satisfaction than a lot of the things I have to do during a normal day. How about you?

A few years ago I discovered the concept of fulling (a.k.a. "felting") wool sweaters and crafting things out of the transformed wool — especially mittens. Actually, I became kind of obsessed with making mittens. It wasn't really the end result — selling them or even having warm hands — that drove me to keep making them,

especially in the heat of a southern summer since I was living in the Deep South at the time. I simply couldn't stop. It was as if my hands were compelled to cut the wool and sew on embellishments or embroider them. I was officially smitten with mittens.

I made so many mittens that I ran out of people to give them to, and seeing as how I was living in Alabama at the time, you might guess that there weren't too many stores jumping at the chance to carry them. Soon I had no idea what to do with the dozens of mittens I was cranking out, so I began to leave them in public places with notes attached to them, hoping they would find good homes.

I would leave my mittens in the freezer section of grocery stores, near

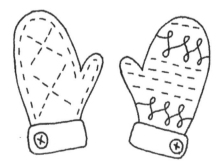

the mailboxes in my apartment complex, in the locker room at my gym, and at my local library. Back then there were no online marketplaces for me to build a store, and though I had a blog, I had no idea what a powerful marketing tool it could have been for me.

If only I'd had the wonderful resources that are available to us crafters today. Though this was just a few years ago, the craft community wasn't at all what it is nowadays. I didn't know of any craft bloggers, and the books at the library weren't the fresh, modern ones obtainable today. Few resources existed for someone like me to help me to grow and develop or even just connect with other like-minded people.

Today, of course, the craft community is thriving, with room for everyone, no matter what your handmade forte. You can easily find kindred spirits who can mentor you, inspire you, help you out of a crafting jam, and offer kind words when you make something wonderful. Our community is so creative, so alive, and so welcoming. The benefits of reaching out to others and making yourself available in turn are almost endless. Just as in any other area in your life, making friends and building community around your passion will be invaluable.

Whatever your personal reason for handcrafting, making things can be not only good for your soul, it can (let's face it) also be good for your bottom line. Selling your crafts is empowering — and collecting money for what you make feels good and, as it turns out, is even easy. These days the demand for handmade goods is high, and as a maker of such things, you're already qualified to meet the need. So many different ways are available to sell your crafts that no matter what your life is like, you can find something that works for you. If you're a people person, craft fairs might be the way to go. If you have the time to manage an online store, you can have a shop that is open 24/7 — and you don't even have to get out of your pajamas if you so choose!

It is my hope that this book will be an encouraging force for you, that you will garner new ideas and new strategies and discover all the places being a crafter can take you.

My Creative Collective

Taking your creativity to the next level is exciting, and to help you along the way, I've asked some of my favorite crafters to join me in welcoming you to our community. These remarkable artisans, artists, and businesspeople make up what I call my Creative Collective. I asked them to share their top tips and experiences in making and selling their wares. They were not only incredibly generous with their time but also willing to be resources for all of us. Some of these folks I chose because I have followed their lives on the Internet for a long time, and they have been a source of great inspiration to me. Others are crafters whose professional work I've admired and knew they could impart some valuable lessons. All of them are experts at what they do, even if that means just being an expert at being a beginner when it comes to selling their work.

Without further ado, I'll introduce you to these talented individuals. A compact list of their websites is included in the Resources section on page 211, and I encourage you to check out their blogs, websites, and online stores. Each of them makes a valuable contribution to the creative community. Not only are they skilled at their crafts, they are skilled at tutorials, podcasting, marketing, design, writing, and working craft fairs. They will provide you with inspiration, motivation, and ideas.

ALISON GORDON

www.sewmaryann.etsy.com
Alison's creations blend sewing, silk-screen printing, and quirky fun. She also runs The Sampler (*www.homeofthesampler.com*) and is a co-organizer of the Bazaar Bizarre (*www.bazaarbizarre.org*). I first met Alison in person when I attended Boston Bazaar Bizarre and fell in love with everything in her booth.

AMBER KARNES

www.7citiescrafters.com

Amber is a graphic and Web designer from Norfolk, Virginia, where she also sews, knits, and takes glorious photographs. I have been reading her blog for many years now, and I'm always impressed by her fearlessness when it comes to crafting. She also started her own craft fair and designs gorgeous websites.

AMY KAROL

www.angrychicken.typepad.com

Formerly a commercial interior designer, Amy lives in Portland, Oregon, where she makes art and writes. Check out her sewing books, *Bend-the-Rules Sewing: The Essential Guide to a Whole New Way to Sew* and *Bend the Rules with Fabric: Fun Sewing Projects with Stencils, Stamps, Dye, Photo Transfers, Silk Screening, and More.* I have been a reader of Amy's for years and was a charter subscriber to her Mailorder project. I find her to be truly inspiring.

ASHLEY GOLDBERG

www.ashleyganddrew.com

Ashley Goldberg lives in Portland, Oregon, where she is an illustrator. She and her partner, Drew, work together to produce all of the goodness you can find at *www.ashleyg.etsy.com*. They are a great example of teamwork, and the very first thing I ever purchased from an online marketplace was from them.

BETSY CROSS

www.betsyandiya.com

Portland, Oregon–based Betsy is an oil and charcoal artist and a photographer, but she is mostly known for being a wonderful jewelry designer. Betsy and I met each other a few years ago, and I'm not surprised by her current success. She is as gutsy and friendly and fresh as her designs.

CAROLINE DEVOY

www.jcarolinecreative.com

Caroline lives in Houston, where she left the business world to start a creative business selling fabric online. I first became familiar with Caroline by following her on Twitter. Once I found out she was a crafty person who used to be an accountant, I knew I needed to have her in my book.

DIANE GILLELAND

www.craftypod.com

Diane produces CraftyPod, a blog and podcast about making stuff, and teaches a variety of craft classes in her hometown of Portland, Oregon. She has written for print and online publications including *CRAFT* magazine, *CraftStylish*, and *Sew Simple*. Back when I discovered podcasts, I immediately looked for craft-related ones.

I found Diane, and now tuning into her show is like hearing from a friend — one who's incredibly knowledgeable about everything (it seems!) related to crafting. She is a Craft Treasure.

ELIZABETH MACCRELLISH

www.squamartworkshops.com
The founder and director of Squam Art Workshops, Elizabeth lives in Sandwich, New Hampshire, with her husband and their three dogs. I first found Elizabeth online many years ago, and I've always been intrigued by her energy and spirit. I was lucky enough to attend the very first Squam Art Workshop, and she was just as great in person as I had hoped.

EMILY MARTIN

www.theblackapple.net
Emily Martin — painter, stitcher, and scribbler — lives and works among the giant fir trees of Portland, Oregon. Together with her partner, Josiah, she runs a cottage industry known as The Black Apple. She loves her kitten, Miette; Little Golden Books; swans; and really good root beer. I knew from the very beginning of this project that I wanted Emily to illustrate my book. I am so happy to have her here.

GRACE BONNEY

www.designspongeonline.com
Grace is the founder and editor of Design*Sponge. She has worked as a contributing editor at *House & Garden,* *Domino,* and *CRAFT* magazines. In addition to Design*Sponge, Grace hosts a series of national meet-ups that help connect women running their own design-based businesses. I heard Grace speak once about the benefits of following your creative dreams and she was really inspiring. Her site is a daily read for me, especially the "Biz Ladies" column.

HOLLY BECKER

www.decor8blog.com
Holly is a writer and interior design consultant who lives in Germany. She is the founder and author of decor8, a popular online destination with over 25,000 daily readers worldwide. Asking Holly to contribute to my book was a no-brainer. She really *gets* the craft community, and her website is a source of inspiration for people all over the world. She has a superfriendly tone, and her posts are always spot on.

JEN SKELLEY

www.jenskelley.etsy.com
Jen Skelley is an illustrator who lives in Massachusetts, and I feel really lucky to have Jen's illustrations in my book. I met her for the first time at a local

craft fair and I've been a big fan ever since. You can check out all of her amazing work in her Etsy shop.

JENNIFER ACKERMAN-HAYWOOD
www.craftsanity.com
Jennifer, from west Michigan, is the producer of the CraftSanity podcast. She was a print journalist for more than a decade and writes a weekly arts-and-crafts column for her home-town paper. Jennifer asks the best questions when she interviews people, and I love her show, which is a must-listen in our house.

JENNIFER JUDD-MCGEE
www.swallowfield.etsy.com
A mixed-media artist and illus-trator living in Portland, Maine, Jennifer shows her work in galler-ies across the United States and in Canada and does freelance editorial work for magazines. She blogs at *www.swallowfield.typepad.com.* I first met her a few years ago at a craft show in Brooklyn, and I've been a collector of her work — which I adore — ever since.

JENNY RYAN
www.homeecshop.com
LA–based Jenny is the creator of Felt Club, a blogger for *CRAFT* magazine and Apartment Therapy in LA, and author of *Sew Darn Cute: 30 Sweet & Simple Projects to Sew & Embellish.*

She also owns and teaches at Home Ec., a crafting workshop and retail space. Jenny is one of the first craft-ers I followed online. Plus, I admire her for pursuing so many different crafty avenues.

JESSICA MARSHALL FORBES AND CASEY FORBES
www.ravelry.com
Husband-and-wife team Jessica and Casey live in Boston with their famous dog, Bob. They started a web-site called Ravelry that has become a huge hit with people who like to knit and crochet. I turned to them for their thoughts about online communities since Ravelry is a really great example of the crafting community at its best.

KAREN WALROND
www.chookooloonks.com
Karen is a Houston-based writer and photographer whose fine-art pieces and projects have been exhibited around the country. She blogs at Chookooloonks and contributes to the collaborative website Shutter Sisters, a photo blog aimed at inspiring and creating community among avid women photographers. Karen is an amazing photographer and was the first person who came to mind when I decided to get professional photo tips for you.

KIM WERKER

www.kimwerker.com

Kim is a writer, editor, blogger, and online community manager. She's the founder of the website Crochet Me and the author or coauthor of six books including *Crocheted Gifts*, *Crochet Me*, and *Get Hooked*. I "met" Kim online through Twitter. She is an excellent resource when it comes to the topics of crafting and technology.

LAURIE COYLE

www.lauriecoyledesigns.com

Laurie is an artist and crafter based in the beautiful Berkshire Hills of western Massachusetts. Her work includes nature-inspired and upbeat paintings, illustrations, mixed media, stationery, and needle-felted and sewn sculptures. Laurie and I met when she was working at an art school, and later we worked side-by-side in a small shop. Now she makes her living as a full-time artist, and it has been a real learning experience for me that someone so close to me could figure things out so well.

LEAH KRAMER

www.craftster.org

Leah is attracted to crafts that are irreverent, ironic, kitschy, or cleverly ecofriendly. Founder of the online community Craftster in 2003, she was also an organizer of the Boston Bazaar Bizarre for seven years and was a founding partner of the hipster brick-and-mortar craft store Magpie in Somerville, Massachusetts. Craftster was the very first place online I found community, and connecting with Leah and her site was like coming home for me. Until Craftster I had no idea there were so many other people like me out there.

LIZ SMITH

www.madeinlowell.blogspot.com.

Liz runs Made in Lowell out of a studio in an old textile mill in Lowell, Massachusetts, where she creates felted and polymer clay accessories and jewelry for craft shows and her Etsy shop, *www.madeinlowell.etsy.com*. When I first discovered Etsy, I looked for people who were nearby, and I found Liz. I emailed her — and we became fast friends. She is a seasoned professional and chock-full of good advice.

MATI ROSE MCDONOUGH

www.matirose.com

Mati is a San Francisco–based artist and illustrator who grew up off the coast of Maine and draws inspiration from both East and West Coasts. Mati has had numerous shows, and has published illustrations in books and magazines. We met at Squam Art Workshops artists' retreat, and she was so friendly that when I decided to write this book, I knew I wanted to introduce my readers to her.

MATT STINCHCOMB

www.etsy.com

In his role as vice president of Community at Etsy, Matt handles the company's community development and strategic community partnerships. Though he never has the time to stock his Etsy shop, Matt is a musician, screen printer, and photographer. I turned to Matt for some marketing and online shop advice management tips for all of you.

MEGAN REARDON

www.notmartha.org

Megan lives in Seattle, where she is part of the Grassroots Business Association and builds websites. She's been publishing findings and ideas at her own website, not martha, since 2001 and ran a small business called The Organized Knitter for four years. Megan's website is a daily must-read for me. Her links for everything from cooking and eating to crafting are an indispensable part of my online life.

MEGAN RISLEY

www.megrnc.etsy.com

Megan lives in Durham, North Carolina, where she designs patterns for her interactive play quilts, handbags,

pouches, cases, and more. She sells her items online, in stores along the East Coast, and at craft fairs. Megan is a seasoned crafter, and her involvement in her local crafts community is inspirational. She sets a good example for crafters everywhere.

NATALIE ZEE DRIEU

www.craftzine.com

Natalie is an author, writer, and crafter in San Francisco. She is the editor-in-chief for Craft (*www.craftzine.com*), and a regular speaker at conferences about the do-it-yourself (DIY) movement and the convergence of crafts and technology. Natalie has also brought her crafting know-how to numerous regional and national TV appearances. Between working for Craft, organizing Maker Faire, and writing a popular blog, Natalie is an excellent resource for all of us.

NICOLE VAUGHAN

www.craftapalooza.com

Nicole lives in Western Australia, where knitting, sewing, and quilting are her main passions. Nicole organizes one of my favorite craft swaps, called back-tack, *http://backtack.blogspot.com*. I always look forward to her blog posts. Her photos are beautiful, and her blog is a treat to read.

PAUL LOWE

www.sweetpaul.typepad.com

A Norwegian by birth, Paul moved to New York City, where he works as a prop stylist — you can see his work in many magazines and books — and creates a variety of crafts as needed by his magazine clients. Paul is one of my personal main sources of online inspiration. His blog is full of great photos, cool projects, and lots of crafty ideas. He makes everything look so beautiful.

TARA SWIGER

www.blondechickenboutique.com

Tara loves to spin yarn, dye fiber, and knit in her Johnson City, Tennessee, farmhouse. She specializes in organic fibers and sells her hand-dyed yarn on her website. I was first introduced to Tara on Twitter, and I wanted to include her because I really admire her honesty and fearlessness. She quit her job in 2009 to follow her dream full-time — and it's working out just great.

YVONNE EIJKENDUIJN

www.yvestown.com

Belgium-based Yvonne is an interior designer, stylist, and photographer. Yvonne also likes to sew and sells popular Japanese craft books through her online store. Check out her website for some of the most beautiful interiors photos online. Yvonne really knows her stuff when it comes to styling and photography. Everything she does is a feast for the eyes.

With the support and incredible wealth of information shared by this group, we're ready to dive into the world of the handmade marketplace. Ready? Let's get creative!

XO, Kari

PART 1

GETTING TO KNOW YOURSELF AND YOUR BUSINESS

BRANDING

Setting Goals

Collecting Money

THE NEXT STEP

Chapter 1

SETTING THE SCENE FOR SUCCESS

The very fact that you're reading this book says that you're interested in taking your handmade experience to the next level. Perhaps you want a second income stream. Maybe you're considering selling your work full-time and leaving your 9-to-5 job behind, but you want to start slowly and test the waters a bit before you take a cannonball-type leap into full-time entrepreneurship. Whatever your reasons, exploring selling your work is an exciting endeavor.

Nothing beats having your work appreciated so much that someone is willing to trade their hard-earned money to own it. (Well, the feeling of coming across your work out in the world when you weren't expecting it is a super-rush, too!) Doing what you love and actually earning money from it is an amazing feeling. Doing work you both enjoy and control while making a living is the best. It's as simple as that. Even if you love your day job, no matter what kind of satisfaction you get from it, the feeling of supporting yourself from something you created can't be beat.

If you're willing to put yourself out there and try something, selling your crafts can be a very rewarding experience. You can make it whatever you want — that is the beauty of running your own business, whether large or small. You get to be in control, and you can change your mind about the way things are happening whenever you want.

Do you like to stay up late and wake up late? You're in luck if you're your own boss because you can set your own hours. You can also determine what your projects and objectives are, and *you* decide how you want to measure your own success.

You'll have the opportunity to hone and develop your skills with your creative whims as your guide. Connecting with a community of buyers and like-minded sellers is a little like choosing your own coworkers. The feedback you get once you put your work out there into the world can feel like receiving a great review from a day job.

You don't need to be an expert at any one thing to make a go of trying new things. You simply need the desire to start something. You can take it anywhere you want after that. You don't have to choose just one thing, either. If your creative heart likes to decoupage and spin wool, then go for it.

For the most part, all you need to start a tidy little business is the desire to create and the desire to sell. If you choose to set up booths at craft fairs during the summer or around the holidays, well, sure, you'll need some extra supplies like a tent and table. But armed with a digital camera and a computer, you could be in business at any time.

Choose Just One Thing? Why?!

If there's one notion that virtually everyone in my Creative Collective agrees on, it's that you don't have to choose just one craft — or even one way of doing one craft — and stick with it forever. In the sage words of whomever it was who said it first: Variety is the spice of life.

All crafts are fair game to me — the only thing in my way from using a supply/medium is time, sometimes the know-how, and sometimes the equipment. I can usually find all three if I am dead set on learning something.
— AMY KAROL

I think however narrowly or broadly you need to define yourself or your work to make the best work you think you can make is the right decision. I personally always have conflicting feelings. I don't want to be a jack of all trades and master of none, but I also don't want to feel stifled.
— ASHLEY GOLDBERG

I don't think people have to choose only one area of focus. I believe all of the arts and crafts overlap and feed into each other and fuel new ideas. There are no boundaries where creativity is concerned.
— MATI ROSE MCDONOUGH

14

Setting Goals

If your schedule is already tight, you may need to consider what you want out of your business before you dig in. Setting some clear goals regarding why you want to sell your crafts will help you make some very important decisions along the way. Do you want to earn enough money to keep your craft habit afloat? Do you want extra income to pay for an annual vacation? Do you want to start a college fund for your kids? Or do you want to quit your day job and craft full-time?

Like anything else in life, your craft business will give you what you put into it. If you choose to have an online store and you want to make a big chunk of change within a year's time, you'll need to be able to devote yourself to making sure that happens. This may require spending a few hours a day updating your online store, spending Saturday mornings packing up your orders, and spending Sundays writing descriptions and uploading quality photos of your goods. Are you ready for that kind of commitment? Is your family?

If you have a family, they have as big a stake in your venture as you do. Are they supportive of your taking on something like this? Talk over your business idea with the people you live with, the people who depend on you. This can be the first step to making sure that everyone will be on board. Having the support of those closest to you is paramount. Your goals in combination with your current day-to-day life will likely affect how much time you can devote to selling your crafts.

Here are some things to think about before deciding that selling your crafts is right for you:

» Why do I want to start selling my crafts?

» What are my monetary goals?

» What does my idea of success look like? How will I know when I've achieved it?

» Do I have enough free time to devote to selling my work?

» Do I have the tools I need at hand to begin selling what I make?

» Do I have a support system in place for taking on this venture?

» What are my biggest fears?

» What excites me the most about starting a business?

Build a Nurturing Space

Where you create can have an impact on the work you do. You know what kind of working conditions work best for you, and you should try hard to ensure that you have the kind of creative space you need. Surrounding yourself with things that inspire you is a good start. If you don't have the space to devote a whole room to your crafty pursuits, you'll need to think outside the box. Can you turn a closet that's currently filled with junk into a craft closet? Or can your china cabinet double as a place to store your craft supplies if you work at the dining room table?

Welcoming Inspiration

What inspires you? Nature? Exercise? Travel? Exploring your town? Window shopping? Inspiration can strike at any time, in any place. One minute you're folding laundry, and the next thing you know, a creative problem that has been plaguing you is solved. A walk in the woods can refresh your mind and body and spirit, and the path you take can lead not just your feet somewhere new but your mind as well. Sometimes when I cook or bake, I find my mind wandering, and the next thing I know, I'm dying for that kitchen timer to sound so I can get into my studio.

Take note of what you're doing when inspiration strikes. Maybe you'll begin to notice a pattern between your good ideas and your activities.

FROM THE CREATIVE COLLECTIVE: YVONNE EIJKENDUIJN

With my basement sewing room I can go crazy and leave fabric cut-offs laying around for a couple of days.

xx xx xx xx xx xx xx xx xx xx xx xx xx xx xx xx xx x xx xxx xx xx xx xx xx xx xx x xx xx xx xx xx x

My husband is a writer, and I'm not kidding when I say he gets out of the shower every day with a new plot twist written out in his head. Carry a small notebook with you everywhere — though perhaps *not* the shower — and take the time to jot down ideas when they occur to you. But make sure your notes are clear enough for you to understand them later. I am still puzzling out a note I wrote to myself a few months ago that says "love to pet animal car." I have no idea what that means or what my intention was, but I wish I did because it sure sounds intriguing!

It's also a good idea to have a camera (or a cell phone with a camera) with you at all times. These days you can get an affordable camera small enough to fit in your pocket, and having one handy is a valuable tool. When you're taking your morning jog, for instance, you might come across a beautiful wildflower that gives you an idea for a piece of jewelry or for a wonderful painting. Inspiration is often unexpected, but it's always welcome.

Set Up an Inspiration Wire

Even the tiniest workspace can host an inspiration wire. Simply hang a length of cord, string, or ribbon, and clip to it whatever strikes your creative fancy. You can use clothespins, bulldog clips or paperclips, or even tape to secure your paper muse to your wire. Make sure you hang the wire someplace where you'll be able to look at it often — maybe above your worktable or even over your kitchen sink.

And an inspiration "wire" doesn't have to be literally a length of wire (or cord). You can create an inspiration wall, an inspiration bulletin board, or even an inspiration collage sandwiched between a piece of Plexiglas and a frequently used table. I happen to have an inspiration scrapbook. As I read magazines or find images on the Internet or look through photos, I clip out or print images that speak to me, and into a box they go. Every now and then I go through the box, and those images that pass the second round go into my inspiration scrapbook.

Working in Small Spaces

My studio is my perfect, lovely, tiny cave. As a little girl, I used to have illusions of setting up my closet as a reading nook, with just a lamp, a few pillows, and a blanket. Now, my studio is truly a respectably sized closet, and I've filled it with buttons, old photographs, a toy piano, stacks of fabric, and handmade and vintage toys, but it still feels like my childhood closet. It's the coziest place I could be. As far as actually drawing and painting, I drag that all over the place; but my computer work, sewing work, and solitude seeking is done in my tiny nook.
— EMILY MARTIN

If your crafting space is limited, don't despair! There are lots of creative solutions to make an organized, mobile work space.

Storage bins, cookie tins, and coffee cans can all be useful when it comes to storing your supplies. Craft them up by covering them in pretty paper, or test out your desire to decoupage on shoeboxes that are now your storage boxes.

Transforming unwanted or unneeded items into something pretty can also be a great way to get your creative juices flowing. If you're short on ideas, working on something for yourself, like covering your magazine storage boxes or turning an old coffee can into a paintbrush holder, may help you get back on your creative track while helping personalize your workspace.

Getting Unstuck

What You Can Do When Inspiration Has Skipped Town and Taken Your Creativity with Her.

Inspiration is at the root of starting and maintaining a great handmade craft business. Sometimes you can be so full of inspiration that you're bursting with ideas and concepts, and you just can't wait to get started. You spend all of your waking moments thinking about your ideas, to the point where normal daily tasks like driving to work or doing your dishes seem to be time wasters. You will not be satisfied until you sit down and get to work. Constructive times like these should be relished because inspiration can be a cruel mistress. Because there will be times, and probably plenty of them, when you sit at your work station and sigh with frustration.

That's when you look around at things you've created before and you wonder, "Why did I make *that?*" or "Where did *that* come from?" Your supplies don't call to you. Your creative flow has dried up, leaving you deserted on the Isle of Nothingness with no hope of rescue in sight. You will be alone in your uncreative world. When this happens, do not despair! You can do lots of things to clear up this unfortunate condition. It happens to the best of us, and you are not alone, my friend.

I find motivation in the simple fact that I get to make art on a day-to-day basis, and I have something to offer the world through that work. I find I am much more productive when I have a selling opportunity like a craft fair coming up.

Window Shop

So you're still stuck. You have gazed anxiously at your inspiration wire to the point where you want to yank it down and strangle yourself with it. What else can you do? Leave!

Go out and absorb the sights in your town. Study the windows of your favorite boutiques. Jot down notes in the little notebook that you of course have in your bag. What catches your eye? A certain color combination? An artful display? The pattern in some beautiful fabric? All of these details can supply you with a new outlook and a new vision.

Look at work that is similar to your own. If you throw clay bowls, see what other people who design clay bowls are doing. Look for new trends and new techniques that you may be able to put your personal twist on. Challenge yourself to do what you normally do just a little bit differently. Learning new things and studying the work of others is a great way to pick up new ideas. Conversely, studying the past of your craft of choice may reinspire you. Take a trip to your local library, and look up, say, the history of embroidery. I bet you'll discover something so old, it is new to you.

FROM THE CREATIVE COLLECTIVE: TARA SWIGER

When I'm inspired by a color, usually in nature, I try to recreate it in a yarn. But when I'm inspired by reading something or soaking up a new city, it impacts me differently. It gives me a renewed sense of vigor and excitement, which usually leads to me challenging myself to do something I haven't tried yet.

Feed Your Artistic Senses

I make a point of always being open to inspiration, so perhaps that's why I'm able to find it virtually everywhere. Some sources are obvious — craft magazines and art and craft books, for example, or craft stores or websites like Etsy — while others may be less so. Seek out museums and galleries for fresh ideas, or go to places you've never been but have always meant to visit, like a historic house with gorgeous gardens. Flea markets, antiques stores, and thrift shops can be endless sources of ideas; look especially for vintage books (particularly old children's books) and ephemera and interesting textiles and wallpapers, both old and new. Search out other crafters' blogs to see what the community is up to. And don't forget to look around you: nature is the best inspiration going! Examine the patterns in rocks or flower petals, shells or a dragonfly's wing. Amazing! Enjoying life's simple pleasures, such as a long bath, a good meal, listening to music, and especially paying attention to your dreams are all wonderful resources.

Get Together with Other Crafters

Sometimes all we need to get us going is other people. Being around other creative types who share your passion can be really rejuvenating. Building community around your craft is one of the biggest advantages you can give yourself. Take a class or join a craft group. There you can learn new skills, make new friends, or simply partake in someone else's joys and sorrows when it comes to living a creative life. Friendship is one of the world's most inspiring things, right?

Inspiration Lost and Found

Everyone has felt deserted by inspiration at one point or another. And everyone is eventually reunited with their motivation. Here's some wisdom from some experts.

All the obstacles I've encountered have been related to figuring how to do something. How can I grow? How can I balance family life with obsessive crafting? There have been no obstacles imposed by people or organizations; it's been internal.

— **TARA SWIGER**

If I am working on a textile design and get stuck, I will look at cookbooks and bake. I never try to get unstuck by going at it directly. I go for a walk, take a shower, or just go out with friends — the worst thing I could do is TRY to be creative when I am not feeling it.

— **AMY KAROL**

Both my craft room and my office at work are filled with images, art, and color that inspire me. I also keep the spaces as clean and uncluttered as possible; otherwise, it's hard for me to focus on the task at hand.

— **AMBER KARNES**

The best way I've found to get unstuck is to dramatically switch gears. If I'm banging my head against a creative project with a growing feeling of desperation and panic in the pit of my gut, it's time to walk the dog or throw in a load of laundry. I need to do other stuff and let the unsticking happen when I'm not paying attention.
— **KIM WERKER**

I need to be surrounded by the things that inspire me, that make me happy, and that I find beautiful to look at. It's all about me, really. In my former home I painted the pantry a bright pink, and people asked me why since nobody was going to see it. But I have to look at it every day!
— **YVONNE EIJKENDUIJN**

I journal and sketch almost daily to capture my ideas so I can keep processing them, and if I'm feeling lazy, bored and lost I can go back and see that they are already there for me. I live in San Francisco and am constantly inspired by the sights in my neighborhood. Even just walking down Mission Street, where all the dollar stores are lining the streets, and noticing the brightly colored plastic bins all lined up, can be an inspiring and important factor in my creative life.
— **MATI ROSE MCDONOUGH**

23

Translating an Idea into Reality

As I noted, inspiration can be found everywhere if you truly look. Now you need to know what to do with that inspiration. Consider a beautiful fall leaf. You might want to match the color to a yarn, or the veins in the leaf may inspire you to attempt or even create a new stitch. That same leaf may inspire you to press it into clay to add texture to a plate you are about to fire in your kiln. The leaf may inspire you to crochet a pair of leaf earrings in wire. Maybe you'll decide to work the leaf into a collage project or make a garland out of felt leaf shapes. That same leaf can compel you to search for leaf-shaped buttons for a skirt you're sewing.

Challenge yourself! Find something — whether it's a page from a fashion or shelter magazine or a photograph of a building in a city you would like to visit or a snippet of fabric with a pattern you adore — and make a list of all the ideas the image gives you. Depending on your flair, your list may look something like this: **Picture of the Eiffel Tower from vacation in France**

IDEAS

- A painting of the Eiffel Tower surrounded by gardens
- A collage featuring the Eiffel Tower with inspirational quotes in the background
- An embroidery project — maybe a small pouch with French words stitched on it
- A silk screen for some T-shirts
- A knitted beret
- A French-themed charm bracelet made from Shrinky Dinks

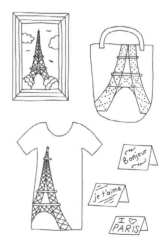

It would be a good idea to record where and when you get inspired. As you keep track of your projects, you'll find it's useful to know each and every detail of what you made and why. For example, if you made a beautiful messenger bag designed with a scalloped edge flap and fabric yo-yos acting like flowers with embroidered stems, perhaps you were inspired by something you recorded in your notebook — maybe a particular flower you saw while on a picnic. If the source of your inspiration is written in your project notes, when you get stuck in the future, you'll find it helpful to see that gardens (or your favorite store, or stargazing) really give you good ideas. Maybe you'll even notice patterns or trends that you weren't aware of before. Bonus!

FROM THE CREATIVE COLLECTIVE: KIM WERKER

I think the greatest creative inspiration comes from seeing other people make things. Sometimes I'm terrified to ask them about what they're doing, but I suck it up and ask anyway. Sometimes I go home and gather some materials and start shooting in the dark to try to figure it out myself. Regardless, sometimes I love it, sometimes I hate it, and sometimes I create something truly horrific. Never, though, do I regret it.

Retreat into Creativity

Consider going on an artist's retreat. Amazing gatherings take place all across the country that accommodate all kinds of interests. It can be expensive, but if you can pull it off, the payback is well worth it. Consider creating something special — if you're a painter, a special painting series; if you're a weaver, unique blue scarves — to raise funds for this kind of inspirational venture. Let your customers know that all the money you collect from these particular items will go to fund your creative vacation.

People who attend The Squam Art Workshops leave with a renewed sense of what they are most passionate about and how vital it is to bring that passion into their daily lives long after the retreat is over.

And one of the coolest things is the friendships that are made here. I know of groups who get together now on a regular basis or spend a special weekend together to keep the magic and connection they made at Squam alive.

Our attendees cannot be defined by age, gender, or geography — but what they all have in common is a desire for more joy, pleasure, and adventure in their daily lives.

I tell everyone to come with no expectations. Each person creates his or her experience. One of our mottos is: Come as you are; leave as you want to be.

— **ELIZABETH MACCRELLISH**

Chapter 2

BRANDING YOUR BUSINESS

As the old saying goes, first impressions last. Think about the image you want to project: What's unique about your craft? Your look and presentation? Your business name? Whom do you want to share your crafts with? What do you want them to know about you and your work? No matter how small you're starting, building your brand before you launch your business can make a big difference in the long run. So think of this chapter as "A Beginner's Guide to Building a Business Image" or "Branding 101."

Your brand is more than just a crafty logo, a catchy slogan, and a great name — although all of those elements are important. Your brand is basically your identity. It is the essence of who you are and what you're selling. It is everything about you and your product. Your lifestyle and the image you project online and in your daily life are all a part of your brand.

Have you ever seen something for sale and immediately thought of someone you know? It could be the perfect color for him or smell like him or have an image on it of something he collects. Maybe you can't even put your finger on it, but you know it is the exact right gift for the person you have in mind. In a way, you were reminded of this person because that particular item matched his personal aesthetic, which in essence is his personal brand.

Branding yourself and your business is a bit like cooking dinner from a recipe. All the little pieces of you — your look, your logo, your creative style, your materials, your company name — all come together in a big pot, if you will, and when combined with each other, produce something that is uniquely *you*.

FROM THE CREATIVE COLLECTIVE: MATT STINCHCOMB

A brand is much more than a logo. Your brand is your overall lifestyle and the overall embodiment of what your business is about. It is really important . . . that you're telling your story. Your story is your brand. You need to know who your audience is and speak to them about what interests them.

Who Are Your Customers?

People buy things for many different reasons. They may need it, they may just plain old want it, or they may need a gift. Often reasons for buying handmade can be very personal. People feel a connection with the product, or perhaps they are making an effort to buy local, and your handmade soap selling at the farmers' market means they won't have to stop at a big-box store on the way home. A buyer may also feel a personal connection with the crafter. If she's drawn to what you make, she identifies with your creations, and with you.

Learning about your customers will help you create your brand. If you know whom you're selling to, you can better know how to communicate with them. If, say, teens are your main customer base, the branding needs to appeal to them. For example, would you use an old-fashioned calligraphy font to reach out to the teen crowd? Maybe — but they might enjoy a fresher, more contemporary style.

Begin the branding process by knowing your target audience.

It's possible that you yourself are your target audience. Lots of us began crafting to fill a void for something we needed. When you look at your crafts, do you see someone like you buying them?

Good Branding

Emily Martin has an online shop called The Black Apple. She also writes a blog under the same name, and Emily has done a bang-up job with her branding. She paints and sews, but she occasionally makes and sells things like paper dolls, postcard sets, and jewelry, which she calls "fancy wearables." No matter what she is creating, it has a look that is very Emily. Her branding carries over to her blog as well. The subjects she chooses to blog about generally come back to the brand she has built. If she is showing her audience her latest batch of her home-baked cookies, they are usually arranged on a vintage plate and photographed with props like fresh flowers or other odds and ends that all speak to who she is and what her business is about. If you order something from Emily you'll get a package that has been hand-stamped with a custom-designed image, and she usually throws in a free goody, like a bookmark or postcard, that also has the look and feel of who Emily is and what she is about. Even without seeing the return address, you know that something from The Black Apple has arrived in your mailbox. Emily has created an overall style that is immediately recognizable. In other words, Emily has created a successful brand.

Branding is a complete and total image. Not just a logo or a color scheme or a certain product line, a brand has to make people buy into the IDEA.
— AMBER KARNES

What's Your Message and Look?

Take a look at what you're projecting out to the world. Do you advertise? If so, do your ads look different every time, or do you use a standardized format so that with a quick glance a customer could immediately tell it was your ad? Is the image of yourself and your business a cohesive one? This can even apply to your personal appearance. When you're at a craft fair, for example, you should ensure that you reflect the brand you've built. If the brand you've cultivated reflects a folksy theme and style, it would be counterproductive to be sitting in your booth at a craft fair listening to death metal, even if it is your favorite kind of music.

Remember, your customers are buying more than that pack of thank-you cards — they're building their own unique lifestyle.

A distinct identity also helps to set you apart from other crafters who are making similar items. Ideally, when shoppers sees something you've made, you want them to immediately think of you. That's what proper branding does. If you're true to yourself and your customers, you'll readily be able to be true to your brand.

Your brand identity touches you personally. It means keeping your personal appearance consistently similar when you are in public representing your business. If every picture of you on your website, Flickr, and Facebook shows you wearing a nice skirt, a scarf, and a beret, this consistency should be maintained when you go to an event associated with your business. Showing up to a public event wearing a funky old T-shirt and sweatpants may be comfortable, but it wouldn't fit the image of you that people already have.

Think about the stores you yourself shop at on a regular basis. Chances are these stores send a clear, consistent message about what they want to sell you. You know what their general selection is like, what their prices are, and what you can expect when you shop there. Their brand is so pervasive that you can identify their ads without even seeing their logo — and if you saw only the logo, you would know the name of the store. That's effective branding at work.

What's in a Name?

What to call your business is a huge thing. You need something that sums up who you are and what you do — and in a manner that will entice people to look at what you're selling and, hopefully, buy.

Look at some big companies, and think what image is conjured up with their names. Best Buy is pretty simple: they're telling you that you'll get a good deal in their store. On what? Well, we don't actually know because they don't tell us, but hopefully it's enough to make you want to go in and check out their wares. Bed Bath & Beyond is a good one because not only do they tell you that they've got stuff for your bedroom and bathroom, the "Beyond" part seems almost inspiring, as if there's a limitless amount of cool things to be found.

That being said, a name like "The Best Baby Quilts in the Whole World" might be nicely specific about what you do, but it's a little wordy. "Best Baby Quilts" would be a better bet. It's short, it tells people what you do, and it retains enough bragging factor to make customers smile. If I was walking around a craft fair and saw a sign that said Best Baby Quilts, I'd stop in. (Be sure that your products measure up to the heightened expectations customers will have after seeing your name, of course!)

On the other hand, if a booth across from Best Baby Quilts sold lovely quilts, but the sign read Suzy's Crafts . . . eh, maybe I'd skip it. Unless the crafts themselves looked interesting enough to grab my attention, based on the name alone, I'd make a beeline for Best Baby Quilts instead. Behold the power of a good name.

Is It Internet-Friendly?

This may sound silly, but keep the Internet in mind when coming up with a name. You want something that's easy enough for people to find while not being too common. If your last name is Brown and you make a lot of different crafts, choosing Brown's Crafts would make it very difficult for people to find you out of the hundreds of thousands of matches the search engine would turn up. Then again, if you made something unusual or unique, like theremin cases, you could get away with using Brown's Theremin Cases. If it's your name that's unusual, then you'll have to figure out if it will work for you or against you: an unusual name means fewer search results, and people will find you easily, but a name that is difficult to type or pronounce may make it hard for people to find you at all.

Leave Room to Evolve

Be sure your company name doesn't pigeonhole you into just one area of crafts, especially if you create more than just one thing. A too-specific name might turn away people who are looking for something specific. Say I was searching for a new handbag. I wouldn't give a second glance to a store called Justine's Jewelry. But what if Justine also makes must-have bags and wallets? Justine's more extensive business might do better with something along the lines of Justine's Creations.

FROM THE CREATIVE COLLECTIVE: **EMILY MARTIN**

I chose The Black Apple in a funny way: One unremarkable evening in 2004, I was making a bunch of handmade felt brooches, and I was thinking of different objects that might make a sweet pin. I thought of a black apple, and as I was steeped in art and English academia at the time, all the symbolism of the apple and the color black were a neat contrast and seemed to suit my sensibility very well. So when I started my cottage industry in 2005, I knew just the name I wanted to use!

People are always changing, and I'm willing to bet that your crafting style and interests have changed along the way. As I mentioned, when I was a kid, I loved creating things from the salt dough my mother would make. Later in school I took lots of pottery classes. In my early 20s I discovered furniture restoration. In my early 30s I discovered the concept of recycling sweaters and had a small business making felted mittens. I have made money from making things for at least 15 years now, and if I had established my business under a name that only reflected my furniture restoration — well, it would probably have been a lot harder to sell my mittens.

Right about now you might be thinking, "Whew! Who knew there was so much to choosing the perfect name?!" If you're stumped, which is pretty common, ask your community for ideas. Your friends and family, people who are familiar with your style and aesthetic can help you brainstorm up the perfect moniker. Try to come up with a list, and if one isn't jumping out at you, put it to a vote. Spend some time saying the name out loud. Imagine yourself answering the phone using the name you're considering. If you find the name difficult to say, so will other people — and that could be bad for business.

Do a Name Search

Once you think you've settled on a name, you need to do a name search to see if anyone else has previously laid claim to the name you want. Do a thorough Internet search for starters. While you're at it, you may want to see if there are any names out there similar to what you're choosing. If your name is Katie and you're thinking of using Katie's Crafts, you might want to reconsider using that moniker if a Cate's Crafts already exists. After you've run through the various search engines like Google and Yahoo, check to see if anyone has trademarked your chosen name with the United States Patent and Trademark Office. You can do a free search at their website.

To see if the domain name for Internet use is taken, check the site Whois.Net. But even if nothing comes up there, it doesn't always mean that your name of choice hasn't already been registered. Try typing it into your browser and see what pops up. If the name you want is obvious, clever, or popular, someone may already own the domain, just waiting for someone like you to come along to buy it from them. However, that won't tell you if someone is already using it with a free blogging site, so I suggest you invest some time checking for your proposed name by adding blogging sites (like "blogspot.com" and "type-pad.com" and so on) to the end of the name. Lastly, check with online selling sites. Use the "search for a seller" feature on sites like 1000 Markets and Etsy to see if another maker is using the name you've decided on.

Once you're sure "your" name is available for online and "global" use, you need to check locally and within your state. Not everybody is doing business online yet, so doing a really thorough search is in your best interest. It would stink if you settled on Portland Pretties, and lo and behold a business using the name was located in your very town or the next one over.

Okay, your chosen name is available. What's next? First of all register it, and file a fictitious-name statement, or "doing business as" (see chapter 3, which covers "DBA"). Also, consider reserving your name on the various websites where you'll want to market yourself, like Facebook, Twitter, Flickr, and any blogging websites you may want to use in the future. Then?

Congratulations! Your business has a name!

Develop a Logo

Almost every business you can think of has a logo (or at least an image of some kind) that represents it. You may want a logo, too. Designing a logo doesn't mean you have to hire a graphic designer — especially if you're not sure what you want quite yet. Do some experimenting yourself. Try using a photo of one of your products, or use a fancy font to create a monogram. Just make sure the font fits in with your branding (if, say, you're all about hand-drawn lettering, using Comic Sans wouldn't be a good fit) and that it will work on any materials you want to print, like stickers and business cards. Make sure it looks good in black and white *and* color, just so you're versatile.

Inspiration for your logo can come from anywhere: the header on your website, a photo that you took of a favorite place (perhaps even your garden) or some vintage fabric you picked up at a tag sale. Keep your customer in mind when designing your logo. Again, you need to be thinking about attracting your target market. If you make items for pets, a logo of your dog or kitty would be perfect.

Choosing all the elements of your brand is fun, even exciting. And don't worry about being literal. If your company name is Blue Bird Baskets, you don't have to have a bluebird and a basket on everything you present to the public. But if you *want* a bird and a basket, think about different ways you can incorporate them into your overall look. For example, instead of using a *bluebird,* perhaps have some other recognizable bird — like a parrot — in a blue hue. Or maybe you can change the birds periodically on all of your materials. Or don't use bird imagery at all, and instead go with a soft old-fashioned look. Whatever the choice, make it *yours.* Let your personality shine through, and your brand will create itself — and customers will feel comfortable with who you are and what you're selling to them.

Defining your image isn't as tough as it may seem. Ask your friends and family for their overall impressions about your style if you're having trouble. They might see something that you don't and the conversation could lead you to an *Aha!* moment that helps you make some decisions.

Chapter 3

ESTABLISHING BASIC BUSINESS PRACTICES

If you already sell what you make, you are already in business. But to be on the up-and-up, you need to make your business legal, and this means defining what kind of business you are. The benefits to doing so are many; conversely, by not complying, you sell your business short and end up hurting yourself. Each state and country has different regulations for owning and operating a business, but there are some general guidelines I can share to get you started in the right direction.

To find out what the exact requirements are for where you live, check your state's official website. Your city, town, or village might have additional laws or regulations, so cover your bases by checking all available local and state resources.

If you run into any snags or problems, and you find yourself needing legal advice, you may want to get an attorney to help you out. If you can't afford an attorney, try researching legal-aid agencies in your area. Many groups and organizations offer free or low-cost help to artists and craftspeople. Your local Small Business Association or chapter of SCORE may also be able to assist you in making your decisions. (SCORE is a wonderful organization composed of business owners and corporate executives — many retired — who volunteer their time sharing their wisdom and lessons they've learned in the business world.)

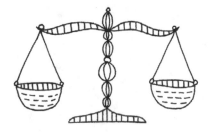

What Kind of Business Are You?

Essentially, businesses fall into three main types, but all three have sub-categories. This means that there are actually lots of choices when it comes to declaring what type of business you are. All have many ins and outs, so taking a good look at what you do and what you want will require some work on your part. This is a pretty important step, and while you can always change your mind, think long and hard about what form of business will be best for you.

No matter what you choose, if you are going to sell something under any name other than your own, you should call up your local county clerk's office and learn how to register your DBA (or Doing Business As) name. This prevents you from using someone else's name or someone from using your name.

Sole Proprietor

A sole proprietor is an unincorporated business. This is the easiest kind of business to get started. You pretty much just need to declare yourself a sole proprietor and then claim what you earn when you do your taxes the following year. You'll need to fill out a special tax form called a Form 1040 Schedule C. If you run your business with no employees, do freelance or contract design, or do craft work, you may be a sole proprietor. As a sole proprietor you are 100 percent responsible for what you do. This means if legal issues arise, like someone gets sick or injured from something you sold them, you alone must take responsibility. It would be possible for customers to sue you personally if they wanted to. Also, if you take out a loan to help your business, you are personally responsible for repaying the debt.

Partnership

So you and your BFF want to go into business together. In that case you may want to consider forming a partnership. This takes more leg- or paperwork than a sole proprietor setup, but all the extra stuff you need to do will help you down the line if one of you wants to buy the other one out or leave the business for any reason. As in any relationship, boundaries need to be acknowledged, and in this case all the assets you and your partner bring to the cutting table need to be spelled out. This means deciding who is responsible for what — as in money coming in and going out of the business — delineating roles and duties, and other business-related minutiae. Hashing out and defining these details is important because as with a sole proprietorship, the law does not separate you personally from your business under a partnership, so all partners can be held legally responsible if something goes wrong.

Limited Liability Company (LLC)

An LLC can be owned by one person or a group of people. The primary benefit of an LLC is you are separated personally from your business, meaning if something were to go wrong, only your business could be sued. While you aren't completely free from liability with this option (hence the name *limited* liability), you are only responsible for what you put into it financially. When it comes to paying taxes with an LLC, you can choose how to be taxed — either as sole proprietor or partnership. If you declare yourself an LLC, expect lots of paperwork on both the federal and state level, along with filing fees. Also, some states don't allow LLCs, so check your local options.

CAN'T DECIDE?

If you've considered all the options but still aren't sure what kind of actual legal business you want to be, I suggest that you consult with members of your community to see how they've handled this issue. This is a great topic to research in the online forums you hang out in. You'll no doubt learn a lot from talking with fellow crafty folk about what kind of business they are and why they made the decisions they did.

The Next Steps

Deciding what kind of business you are is the first step. If you opt for anything other than a sole proprietorship, the government will assign you a Tax ID number, also known as an Employer Identification Number, or EIN. Your EIN helps the government track where you sell your goods and how much you're making. If you begin to sell wholesale to boutiques or stores, you'll include your EIN number on all of your invoices.

After you've decided what category of business you want to be, you'll have to choose an annual accounting calendar. This just means you choose a system that goes along with your business declaration that determines when you pay your taxes to the IRS. You can choose the standard calendar, January through December, which you may find easier because it is the system you are used to with your personal taxes, or a fiscal calendar, which usually runs from October through September of the following year.

Now that you've made the basic decision, you'll probably need to get an accountant involved, and you need to set up your business accounting system. This is a bit different from your inventory system, and if you can set up your system right away — and manage to keep up with it — when it comes time to file your taxes, you'll be way ahead of the game.

Bookkeepers and Accountants

Depending on the size and complexity of your business, you may also need the help of that organizational whiz, a bookkeeper. How does a bookkeeper differ from an accountant? A bookkeeper records the accounts or transactions of a business, your income and expenses that your accountant then utilizes to prepare your taxes and other financial records. Either can help you set up all of this and give you tips that will help start a filing system as well. Everyone is different, and everyone has various strengths and weaknesses. Personally, I am awful when it comes to filing things properly and keeping track of paperwork. Software is available that can help you with this, and your local community college or adult learning center probably offers bookkeeping or accounting classes that you may find helpful.

If you decide to hire someone to help you manage your numbers year-round or just help you set up your system and give you some pointers, you'll need to interview them. Remember, this person will be working for you, and you need to make sure you understand what his services are and how much it will cost you.

Here are some questions you might want to ask your prospective accountant or bookkeeper:

➤➤ Has she ever worked with a business like yours? Make sure you accurately describe the scope of your business to her. You want to know if she has experience with businesses of your size, duration, number of employees, and the like.

➤➤ What are his rates, and how are they calculated? By the task? By the hour? When will he invoice you? Does he require you pay for his services quarterly, weekly, or monthly?

➤➤ What will she need from you and when? All of your receipts monthly? Quarterly? Yearly? Copies or originals? Will she accept e-mailed scans?

If you are interviewing a firm, ask who specifically will be assigned to your account and how often he will need to meet with you. Also, ask what your time with him will be like. Will you be able to call or e-mail and ask questions whenever you think of one, or will he want you to keep a running list that you bring with you during your scheduled face-to-face meetings?

➤➤ What kind of software will she use, and does she recommend you use the same?

➤➤ Would he recommend you get a separate bank account for your business?

A dedicated business account will help you with your recordkeeping. A separate account will make it loads easier for you to keep track of what is coming in and what is going out, plus help you budget accordingly. It will make tracking your credit-card sales and your shop fees easier. You will be

able to see what you spent on supplies as well as simplify find business-trip expenses to craft fairs. Lastly, paying yourself out of this account will make it easier to keep track of your salary, and it will also help you do your monthly statements more quickly.

Check with your bank to see what kinds of information they'll need from you when opening a business account. You may be required to show proof of your DBA and other licenses and paperwork as well. Bottom line: Think about getting a business account as soon as possible.

Recordkeeping

Owning a business means keeping records. Anything that has to do with your business — supply receipts, phone calls charged to your cell or home phone, your mileage — is important when it comes to your taxes. Save everything, and file it immediately. If down the line you think you may have a question about something you've saved (like you buy buttons from an antiques dealer, and the receipt they give you is hard to read), mark it. Just be sure that you save everything, and you understand it all. Recordkeeping and keeping track of every single business-related expense is the only way you will know with any certainty if you're actually making a profit and that you don't pay more taxes than necessary on that profit.

Scan your receipts into your computer and save them.

Keep all of your records for at least seven years — longer if it makes you feel more comfortable. The IRS can audit your records for up to six years past, which is why you always should have seven years on hand (including the current year). Occasionally the IRS can audit you no matter how long it has been. For example, if you didn't file taxes 10 years ago, they could come after you now. However, keeping your paperwork and returns in a box for at least seven years, provided you did everything you were supposed to do, should be enough. When the seventh year passes, shred your documents, and move on.

Collecting Money

When you're collecting money, there are pretty much only three ways to do it: cash, check, or credit card. With your online shop, you are probably restricted to what your host allows you to accept: in most cases, PayPal. However, when you are out and about selling at craft fairs or dealing with wholesale accounts, credit cards and checks will also figure prominently into the mix.

Each state has laws and rules about collecting taxes. To know what you should be charging for taxes either in your shop (real or virtual) or at craft fairs, check with your state and your town. There may be rules for both that you need to factor into your pricing.

If you accept personal checks from customers, remember that checks will take longer to clear at your bank, sometimes up to seven business days, which means it will take longer for you to actually get the money in your hot little hands. Extend that time if you accept checks through the mail because, of course, you have to wait for them to arrive.

Accepting credit cards can be a little more work and will require a small investment on your part, but it will surely pay off in the end.

Accepting credit cards will likely boost your sales, especially when you're selling in public. To do this you need to set up a merchant account with the company of your choosing. Setting up a merchant account simply means that you enter into an agreement with a company that will process your credit-card sales for you, either over the phone or through a secured system using their website. The two most popular ways for you to accept credit cards in person are either with a tabletop imprinter or by calling in your customer's credit-card information on the spot. Also, you can now sign up with a service through companies like ProPay or Innovative Merchant Solutions that gives you the ability to charge a customer's credit card or debit card at a time when it is convenient for you.

When opening a merchant account you need to keep several things in mind. First of all, these companies do not work for free. They make their money by charging you fees, and those fees can add up. They can charge you a monthly fee for using their service, even if you didn't use it that month at all. They also may charge you a cancellation fee if you decide to no longer use them, and they will absolutely charge you for each completed transaction. They can also charge you based on the kinds of credit cards you accept. Some companies may charge more for accepting less common credit cards like Discover or American Express. Other charges to look out for are fees for receiving your statements, processing fees on top of transaction fees, and fees for refunding a customer's money. Research each company carefully, though, and you shouldn't encounter any unpleasant surprises.

An imprinter can be purchased either from your bank or from an online merchant who sells them. You'll need to get something called a custom plate, which usually has five or

······· Credit Card Tips ·······

➤ You can usually get set up with an imprinter (manual credit-card machine, sometimes called a "knuckle buster"), including a custom plate and sales slips, for under 50 dollars.

➤ If you choose to call in credit cards at a fair, be mindful of people waiting for your attention while you're on the phone. This is another reason to bring a friend with you!

➤ Always write down your customer's phone number on the sales slip. Once in a while you may have trouble reading a digit on the carbon imprint, and you may need to contact your customer to verify their credit card number.

so lines of your business information. These machines use carbon paper, so you get a copy of the sales slip as does your customer. These sales slips can be bought at all kinds of places that sell office supplies.

Pricing Your Work

How much is that handmade dog bed in the window? Pricing your work can be a challenge, and there are many different schools of thought on the best way of going about it. The bottom line (pardon the pun) is to ask for whatever you are comfortable with. If it takes you only 10 minutes to woodburn a sign for someone's lake house, and you feel that it's worth $500, that's what you should charge. Or if $50 feels right, go for that number. In the end, you need to make the money you want to make, and you can make sure that happens by charging what you're most comfortable with. But that comfort-level figure can seem awfully elusive.

How the public determines value, what your competition charges, and your costs are a few deciding factors. There's a whole lot more to it, of course, but we'll start there for now. First of all, how do we determine the value of a product? I'll use a painting as an example. You are an amazing painter, right? You know that you can sell a large painting for $500, and prints of the same painting go for $25. However, you then discover that another painter has priced her work for a lot more, but when you raise *your* prices, your work doesn't sell. Why?

A part of it could be the perceived value of your work. The other artist may be able to command a higher price because she has been around a lot longer than you and has a larger audience. Possibly she has exhibited her work in galleries across the country, and because she is more well known than you, people expect and are willing to pay more for that artist's work. Even if you both paint vivid landscapes that bring a tear to the viewer's eye, her work is deemed more valuable based on factors like reputation, a résumé featuring various galleries, or even a lot of good press. The public is willing to pay more because they feel they are getting more, even if the actual work is similar.

But it's not only having an established name that can raise the perceived value of your work. If you create knitted goods, you can explain that your work is worth the money you're asking by talking up your process and materials. If you use only the best organic wool, dye and spin it yourself, then knit an original design, those elements could very well raise the value of your work in your customer's eyes. Let people know why your work is valuable and how much work you put into what you make.

You can get a good idea of your perceived value by checking out your competition and comparing your work with the work of others. Say you're a maker of dog beds. Look at sizes, and see how they compare to yours in price. Or you can look for dog bed manufacturers who use the same types of materials as you or have the same look and feel as yours. Also look for products that have something in common with yours but aren't too similar. By that I mean all dog beds, big and small and in between. Take note of what they are selling for, how many have been sold (if you can figure that out), and how their maker describes them. Plus read their feedback, and see what customers like or dislike about the products.

Use this information to make sure your product is priced appropriately. Perhaps you'll find you are underpricing your goods, or maybe your sales are slow because a similar product out there sells for a lot less than yours. Studying up on the competition can help you decide the best price for what you make.

When you're studying up on the competition ask yourself the following:

- What do my product and this one have in common?

- What sets mine apart? How is mine unique? Better? Worse?

- If I was a buyer comparing this other product with my own, what would strike me as the primary differences? What would be the choices I'd need to make between the two before I spent any money?

- What can my competitor's feedback tell me about my own product?

Determining Your Cost of Goods

Knowing how much your product costs you to make and sell is essential in determining retail price. This includes everything that goes into what you make. For example, the cost of making a fabric wallet can be broken down in several ways, depending on how you source your supplies. These are:

Materials to construct the wallet, including:

- Fabric (includes delivery cost)

- Snaps

- Thread

- Interfacing

- Label (of your company name)

Selling costs for your wallet, including:

- Listing/advertising costs

- Online banking fees

- Shipping tissue paper, sealing stickers, etc.

- Padded envelope or mailing box

- Postage

Note that this list does not include your time — neither actual crafting time nor the time you spent sourcing the supplies, the time you spent driving to the post office to mail it, and the time you spent uploading the article to your store. You must determine what your hourly worth is, and add that to your selling price.

Determining Your Retail Price

Now that you have a base cost for your product, you need to decide how much you can mark it up for retailing.

If a spool of thread costs you $2, you shouldn't charge the full two bucks to the cost of a single wallet. Try to make your best guess as to how much of the spool you use to actually sew the wallet. You may end up estimating the thread costs you somewhere around five cents per wallet.

Let's say you determine that the wallet costs you $5 to make. That five bucks covers your materials, your labor, and the basic costs of being in business. One formula you could use is a 2.5 formula: multiply your base cost by 2.5 and consider that your retail price. Multiplying $5 by 2.5 is $12.50, and you could think of the breakdown this way: the first $5 reimburses you for making the wallet, the second $5 makes you enough money to make another wallet and keep your business going, and the $2.50 is money you could put toward developing another product, like a matching business card holder.

Now look at the market. When you find items like yours, how are they priced? If you find that wallets of a similar size and style are also priced at $12.50, you might want to drop your price a dollar or two to make them competitive. If your wallets feature something really unusual and stand out from the pack, you might want to raise your price.

Something else you'll want to figure out is your wholesale price for doing business with retailers. A wholesale price is more than the base cost, but less than the retail price. In case of your wallets, you'll want to sell them to retailers for more than $5 and less than $12.50. That means you'll get less money than if you sell them yourself, but in return, someone else has taken on the responsibility of advertising and selling your wallets — leaving you free to create and make more!

This example is just one method to figure out what you should charge. Talk to your crafty community for more ideas.

Do not underestimate the value of your work. If you undercharge, you hurt not only yourself but other crafters who are a part of your community.

Wisdom from Betsy Cross

In the very beginning [when I started Betsy & Iya Jewelry], I decided I wanted to sell as much as I could to boutiques and (preferably) wholesale rather than consignment. Generally, my sales tactic is simply exposing buyers to my lines. I've been fortunate enough that my lines tend to sell themselves once clients have a chance to see them.

I was somewhat familiar with the whole pricing game because I had worked for a short bit as a jewelry sales representative. I became a sponge and retained all of that insider business info, such as if you undersell your wares from the start, you might never be able to sell wholesale without raising your prices and raising some eyebrows from loyal retail customers. I did

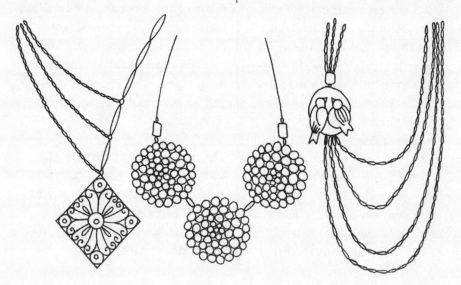

so much research before I actually priced my first piece. Searching for answers to questions like, "What do other comparable designers charge for their wares? How much do I want to pay myself per hour? How much would people *actually* pay for this?" I eventually found a pricing calculator that I really liked. When I price a new design, I consider perceived value, the time it takes me to reproduce a design, and my general price points ($19–$79 retail). For a wholesale account to be successful for both the retailer and me, the price of each piece must allow us both to make a fair and reasonable profit for our time and efforts.

My retail exists because I met an awesome woman who is also a jewelry designer, and I asked how in the heck she has so many Etsy sales. She said one word (actually two): "My blog." Was she ever right! Beyond increasing sales, my blog friend connections have also increased my resource pool. There is a huge group of generous people I know through the blog world that I'm able to run ideas and questions by. The handmade–blog community *rocks*! Beyond that, put money into marketing. It's worth it! You'll get it back times ten!

It's incredibly exciting to see my designs walking down the street. And when customers take the time to write me to describe how often they wear their piece or how beautiful they feel in it — that's it right there; that takes the cake. Those moments are really what keep my business rolling.

Sales: To Have Them or Not to Have Them, That Is the Question

The flyers in Sunday papers all seem to be screaming the same thing: **SALE!** The big-box stores seem to be having sales every week, but when should the handcrafter have a sale? The short answer: It depends.

The main reason to have a sale is to sell more of your inventory. While this seems like a good enough reason, many factors should be taken into consideration when having a sale. The first and usually foremost in everyone's mind is, "I wanna make more money!" Oddly, that *isn't* a good enough reason. However, if you are finding that some of the items on your online store aren't selling at all, you could benefit from a sale.

If you sell your products online, browse around and see how other crafters selling similar products are doing. On Etsy, for example, you can look at the number of items sold by a shop and get a picture of what they're selling. If their similar product is flying off the virtual shelves while yours isn't moving, compare your prices. If they are undercutting you on price, that could be a reason.

Another reason could be the popularity of the other crafter. Does she have a popular website, blog, podcast, or videocast? Or was she recently featured on a popular website, blog, podcast, newspaper article, TV show, or the like? Wider exposure could certainly explain their higher sales.

How do you compete against that? Simply lowering your prices might not drive any extra sales to you because those drawn to your type of product are hearing about your competitor through her increased publicity and already are buying from her. Your best bet would be to increase your marketing efforts to steer more traffic to your sites.

But let's say your competition isn't selling much of anything, either. Look into outside factors. Maybe your woolen mitten-and-hat combo isn't selling because it's July, or maybe it's toward the end of winter, and everyone has already stocked up on their winter warmers. In either of these cases, you may want to consider putting those items on sale.

This brings up a good point of when to put seasonal items on sale. You should be tracking your sales, and if you aren't looking at spreadsheets, you probably at least have a pretty good idea of how often you sell what. Say you're selling an average of five mitten-and-hat combos per week in December. You notice in mid-January those numbers go down to four a week. While that's a 20 percent reduction in sales, I would still hold off for a few weeks to see if it's an actual trend or just an anomaly. But say in early February you notice that you're only shipping one, maybe two hat-and-mitten combos a week on a fairly consistent basis — and have been since mid-January. You check out your competition, and notice it's the same for them, but they haven't reduced their prices yet. Now's the time for a sale. The end of winter is fast approaching, and you're not going to sell very many more hat-and-mitten combos again until November, so advertise it loud and proud: **SALE!** If you've done your homework and have a good marketing system in place, you'll get the word out and sell out the rest of your hat-and-mitten combos for the season.

Hiring Help

On your path to fame and fortune selling your handmade wonderfulness, you may find that you need some help. There is no shame in hiring out certain jobs that you just can't or don't want to do on your own. No need to try to be a crafty superperson. In some cases hiring someone to do tasks for you can even save you money in the long run. Paying a bookkeeper $20 an hour for two hours a month to handle your money frees up two hours that you could spend designing something new that will make you more money, or cranking out four new brooches that you can sell for 50 bucks a pop.

If you can't afford to hire help, you may be able to afford to get guidance. If you belong to a community organization, consider chipping in to ask the professional of your choice to address your group. Collect questions ahead of time, and get them to the speaker so that he or she can best address the collective's needs.

Professional Helpers

Following are some professionals whom you may require help from on your handmade journey.

ATTORNEY/LAWYER

You may need to seek advice from a legal professional at some point or another. Maybe you need help understanding a contract that you've been offered if you accept freelance work. Or maybe you feel like a copyright of yours has been infringed upon. Look for local legal organizations that may offer help to creative professionals at reduced costs or sometimes even for free. Also, be sure to check your local Small Business Association office or other small business resources in your area. Many of them present free or affordable workshops and classes to help the community understand legal issues.

DESIGNER

You might reach a point where you feel like you need to hire out some of your design needs. Consider using a graphic designer who could help you with your branding or a Web designer to design your website or blog.

BOOKKEEPER OR ACCOUNTANT

Maybe you need some guidance in record keeping or you just want someone else to crunch the numbers and/or do your taxes. Again, check with your local small-business groups to see if they can point you in the right direction. Talk to other small-business owners you know; even if they aren't crafters, they most likely use someone to help them out.

PUBLICIST

A publicist can help you reach the media if you have some really big news to share. Hiring a professional to help you spread the word can be more cost-effective than trying to do it yourself. A publicist will already have media contacts, and it would take you a long time to develop a list as comprehensive as hers will be.

MARKETING FIRM OR MARKETING CONSULTANT

Getting some professional guidance with your branding and your marketing strategies can't hurt. These folks will be up on the latest trends and marketing techniques and can give you the best advice.

OTHER CONSULTANTS

Virtually any field has consultants available for hire who are often experts in their chosen subjects. If you can think of a problem, most likely you can find someone willing to consult or guide you through it.

INTERN

An intern is essentially an apprentice, a student of a particular discipline who will often work in exchange for on-the-job training. Interns are looking to get the inside scoop on the career path of their choice. You can find willing interns through local arts organizations or schools in your area.

Before you hire someone, make sure you check their references. Also make sure there is a clear understanding between them and you when it comes to what you are paying for. Be upfront about your needs, and don't be afraid to ask lots of questions.

FROM THE CREATIVE COLLECTIVE: MATI ROSE MCDONOUGH

Within the last year my business has grown to a place where I now need an assistant or intern because I have so many wholesale and Etsy orders to balance with creating new work.

In addition to being the owner of the fabulous online store J. Caroline Creative, Caroline Devoy is also an accountant and therefore someone who's more than qualified to give expert advice from both sides of the business coin. She was kind enough to impart words of wisdom about all things financial.

What kind of receipts should I be saving? Why?

Save every receipt related to your business. Everything. E.V.E.R.Y.T.H.I.N.G. Anything you paid for your business, save the receipt. If you aren't sure if it is for your business, save it, anyway. If the IRS decides to audit your return (not likely, but it does happen), you want to have the appropriate documentation of your expenses. And you should keep that information for three years after you file your tax return.

I know I should track my mileage, but what if I drive to the art-supply store and end up not buying anything? Should I still log it?

If you went to the art-supply store looking for things for your business, yes, that mileage is deductible. If you go to a craft fair and don't sell anything (ouch!), that mileage is deductible. The IRS doesn't care if the trip was successful, just that it was for your business. You can deduct a standard amount per mile (it's adjusted periodically for inflation; your accountant will know the current rate) for business purposes. The IRS requires this log be in writing, so keep a little calendar in your car, and write down every time you drive somewhere for business. If you wrote down the trip but didn't write down the mileage, look it up on Google maps.

Note that when you are deducting standard mileage rate, you may not deduct gas or other car expenses such as repairs or insurance. Those are computed as a part of the standard mileage rate. You may, however, deduct tolls and parking.

How about meals? If I have coffee with my best friend, and we talk about my online shop or our favorite knitting patterns, is that coffee a write-off? What if it wasn't coffee but many cocktails, instead?

Yes, it is deductible, but the IRS got tired of those three-martini lunches being used as a tax deduction, so the deductible for meals and entertainment is now limited to 50 percent: if you spend $50, you can deduct $25. And you better have the receipt, and you better write who you were with and what you talked about on the back. Just in case. But I would make your friend buy her own.

In general, what do I need to record and how?

A good rule of thumb is that any time something hits your PayPal account, your bank account, your credit card, or cash changes hands, it should be recorded. How you choose to record these [transactions] is up to you. You could do something as basic as print your financial statements (from PayPal, your bank, and so on) and note beside each item what it was for. Or you could use a software program like QuickBooks. The advantage to using accounting software is that the categories total automatically rather than you having to add each sale or deduct each expense manually.

What kinds of things will an accountant want from me?

He will expect you to provide him with all your accounting information. If you want to save yourself some money, bring a summary of your income and expenses (in a ledger or a printout) so that he doesn't [have to tally your receipts] himself.

What exactly qualifies as a write-off?

A write-off, which is the same as a tax deduction, is any item that you can deduct from your income, thereby reducing your taxes. Which means that any expense that is ordinary and necessary to your business is deductible according to the IRS. Some things not to forget:

- Office supplies (paper, toner, pens, etc.)

- Cell phone if you need it for your business (which many people do since they don't have a landline for their business)

- Internet connections at your house if you work from home

- Mileage

- Selling fees incurred for online stores (such as Etsy)

- Advertising costs, online or off

- Booth fees (and any display items you purchase, such as fresh flowers, tablecloths, and the like)

- Credit card charges, bank fees, PayPal fees

Items that have "lasting value" — i.e., they are not used up in the process of making goods — are considered assets. And since they are assets, you must usually depreciate the value of the asset over a period of time. The IRS created a system called MACRS (Modified Accelerated Cost Recovery System), where you take a specified percentage of the asset's cost as a deduction every year of its life — usually five or seven years. Examples of assets include digital cameras, laptops, printers, scanners, and any equipment you might need to produce your product. For example, you purchase a digital camera for $1,000. It has a seven-year life under MACRS, so in the first year you would be able to deduct 14.29 percent of [the camera's] value, or $142.90. However, if you didn't purchase more than $800,000 in assets during the year *(cough)* and your business made money, you can deduct the entire purchase price up to $250,000 under something called Section 179. Great for small businesses as you don't have to track the depreciation, and you can get a nice write-off on your taxes immediately.

Are all craft supplies, even ones that we don't end up using in items that are for sale, write-offs?

This is a little complicated. If you buy a few yards of fabric because you think it will make the greatest-ever handbag, but then you make one and realize it made the worst-ever handbag, then write off that fabric. I use an expense category called "New Product Development" because that sounds better than "Crap I Bought That Didn't Work Out." However, if you bought 200 yards of fabric and either haven't made it into purses yet, or the purses haven't sold yet, that fabric would be considered inventory and would not be written off until the items are sold.

What exactly is inventory?

Inventory is basically goods held for resale. So if you sell felted mittens, your inventory includes mittens and yarn. Tracking inventory is important as you are not allowed to deduct as expenses the items that you haven't yet sold. Here is how you can compute inventory: Total up all the money you spent on purchasing and making product for the year; call this Number A. Then count how many items you have not sold (your inventory), and multiply it by your per unit cost (Number B). Subtract B from A, and you get a number known as Cost of Goods Sold, or COGS if you are really cool. That is the amount you get to deduct. Simple, yes?

How do I know if I really need to hire someone to help me?

If you feel comfortable preparing your own tax returns, you may just want to hire someone to review the return before you file. But even if you hire someone to prepare your monthly financials (usually the smallest time frame for which financials are prepared), you need to be sure you understand what she prepares. That information helps you make business decisions, and if you don't understand the information, it can't help you.

Whom you hire should be based on two things: does he or she work with other businesses your size (and are those clients happy with the work), and do you feel comfortable with this person. Oh, and know [in advance] what the charge will be.

Should I invest in accounting software? If so, what are some good choices?

Some businesses can survive pretty well on paper if they don't have a lot of transactions. However, if you are selling a lot of goods on Etsy or from an online store, you probably want the ability to print customer invoices and track your expenses. Plus that information is added up instantly. So, for example, you can total up your spending for advertising any time with no effort.

The software programs all do about the same thing, so I would look for cheap. And the cheapest thing I can think of is free. QuickBooks (www.quickbooks.com) offers a limited version of their Simple Start package for free. Their other software solutions are in the range of $99 to $199, so the investment is not huge. The nice thing about QuickBooks is that they have so thoroughly saturated the small-business accounting market, every accountant can use the data, and it won't be hard to find user forums and other resources for help.

What is "profit"?

Profit simply means that your income exceeds your expenses. So the magic formula is income should be greater than expenses.

Should I seriously get a separate bank account for my business?

If it is really a business and not a part-time hobby, then yes. I'm going to just make up a number for reference: If you think your sales for the year will exceed $2,500, it's time to set up a separate bank account and separate credit card. If your sales are less than that, you are probably fine keeping it with your personal stuff.

Can the IRS claim that this is a hobby and not a business?

Yes. If your business is deemed to be a "hobby" by the IRS, not "an activity engaged in for profit," you may never deduct a loss from your business (where expenses exceed income), should you incur one. If you make money the last three out of five years, the IRS will assume your activity is for profit. If that is not the case, the burden of proof lies with you to prove that you are conducting the activity for profit and not as a hobby. To prove your case, the IRS will consider how you operate the activity — do you treat it like a business? — as well as other factors.

My accountant gave me my financials: an income statement and a balance sheet. What are they?

Financials, or financial statements, refer to the accounting documents that report on a business's financial health. The statements usually include at least a balance sheet and an income statement. A balance sheet is a long-term record of the health of the company — basically a snapshot of all the activity for the life of the company. The balance sheet is where you will see how much cash the company has, its inventory, its assets, and its debts. The income statement is for a specific period of time, so it resets itself at certain intervals. The most common periods for an income statement are monthly and year-to-date, usually shown side by side. The income statement is where you will see the amount of revenue (income) earned for that period as well as the expenses for

that period. The bottom line of the income statement is either the profit or loss of the business for that particular period.

I'm an Internet business, so I don't have to collect sales tax, right?

Wrong. As a business, you are responsible for collecting sales tax for any state in which you operate. So if you operate your business in Ohio, any sales made and shipped within Ohio (even via the Web) are subject to sales tax. (It depends on the state and your sales volume as to how often you will file. You could be required to file sales taxes monthly, quarterly, or annually.)

As a general rule, any state in which you are physically present for your business will subject you to that state's sales tax. So if you physically attend craft fairs in other states to sell your items, you are now subject to that state's sales tax. Your business is in Ohio, but you travel to Illinois for a craft show. You should now be collecting sales tax in Illinois and submitting a sales tax return in Illinois. But using a third-party carrier such as UPS or FedEx to deliver to another state does not subject you to that state's sales tax.

Do a Web search for your particular state, and you should find an application for a "Sales Tax Permit." File the permit, and the state will give you information on sales tax rates and the frequency and method of filing your sales tax returns.

One element about sales tax that is often misunderstood is the exemption from sales tax. If customers tell you they are exempt from sales tax because they are reselling the items, the customers must provide you with a document, usually called a resale certificate, stating that they are exempt. Otherwise, you are still responsible for collecting tax from them. (And don't be surprised if the customers stomp their feet in disgust and tell you that isn't true.)

On the flip side, if a vendor doesn't collect sales tax from you and should (because the items are not being resold), you are still responsible for paying the tax, now called a use tax. This is a common problem with vendors from whom you buy multiple items. You provided them with a resale certificate, so they no longer charge you sales tax on the items you buy from them. That is fine for the items that you resell or the supplies going into items for resale. But it's not okay for items you consume in your business, such as paper, printer toner, and the like.

Many vendors will ask you for a copy of your sales tax certificate before quoting you wholesale pricing. Businesses use this as an indication that you are a "real" business and not just a consumer trying to get better pricing. So you want to get one of those permits sooner rather than later.

One more thing on sales tax . . . . small businesses tend to panic about being audited by the IRS, though the chances of that are pretty low. But your chances are not slim for being audited for sales tax. States aggressively pursue sales-tax collections and often target small business because they are easy. So know the rules for your state, and comply with them because it will save you the headache of writing your state a big check later.

Chapter 4

MARKETING BASICS

O kay, you have created *the* most beautiful handmade items. Your workshop — or spare room — is filled with your fabulous pieces. Now what? The answer is obvious, right? You have to sell your stuff. And this is where many artisans run into the proverbial brick wall. After speaking with crafters from all over the world about starting a business, I've learned that the one thing that most mystifies you ingenious folks and causes you to bury your heads in your yarn baskets is marketing. And yet marketing can be so creative and fun, it's truly a big ol' shame that it's so scary to you.

Marketing Defined

Let's start with the definition of marketing: Marketing is simply how you sell what you make. You make things, you want to sell them, you need to market them. It's as simple as that. You can be the best painter in the world, but if you can't sell your paintings, you'll never have that feeling of satisfaction that comes with being financially successful from selling your work.

Sure, the feeling of satisfaction you get from making something amazing is undeniably terrific. But the satisfaction you get from sharing your amazing work with the world and selling it so that you make money — well, that's something else entirely. And don't forget that ultimately it will enable you to buy more supplies and paint more paintings.

Marketing is one of the keys to your success, and I promise it can be fun. You already know that you're artistic and talented; marketing uses those same skills to spread the word about what you do. It's reaching out to your audience and inviting them to interact with you — to purchase your work, to converse with you about your creations, or to get excited enough to spread the word about you and your craft.

Essential Marketing Materials

As a savvy crafter, you should never be without certain basic marketing materials so that you're ready to promote yourself at any given moment. Say you're standing in line at the grocery store, and someone comments on the lovely hand-sewn bag you're carrying. You'll tell her you made it, of course, and in fact you have a business selling your hand-sewn creations. She'll ask if you have a business card, and you'll reach inside your amazing purse for your card case and hand one over. Right?

Wait! What if you don't *have* a business card?! Surely you don't expect all those admiring strangers to remember your name or your website address or your phone number, do you? Yes, business cards are an essential marketing tool for anyone in business. The others are:

- Promotional postcards
- Nametags and stamps
- Photographs of your creations

Marketing materials go beyond what you carry on your person. You need to take every single opportunity that comes your way to promote your work.

Let's look at these marketing essentials in order . . . .

Business Cards

Business cards are the very least of your essential marketing materials. You can get them cheaply, and you can control how they look. You can either design and print them yourself (on your home printer), or you can get them custom designed and printed. Some websites will even print your business cards for free in exchange for printing their own business information on the card somewhere; you simply upload an image to a website, and voilà! Business cards will be on the way to you.

How your business cards look is up to you. However, you should consider your overall branding (see chapter 2), and make sure your cards fit in with the image you've decided to go with. If you use photographs of your work on everything, consider a card with a photograph of your signature item. If you use a logo, you should have that on your business cards.

No matter what design you go with, make sure you include all of your basic information so that potential customers can find or purchase your work — which is, after all, the goal. That includes your e-mail address and the URL of your blog, website, and online shop if you have one. These days it's also appropriate to include your Facebook name or your Twitter handle.

If you make ecofriendly products, consider using recycled paper to further promote your message.

Matt Stinchcomb of Etsy

As vice president of community at Etsy, Matt knows all about selling tools and strategy. Here he shares some of his knowledge.

On the importance of marketing:

Marketing doesn't mean big ads on television or in magazines. Marketing, to put it simply, is how people perceive you and your business. Any way that you put yourself out there is marketing. It is how you communicate. Whether that is by an advertisement or a blog post or a tweet, marketing is the message you send to the world about you and what you're selling.

On the importance of customer service:

Create a positive experience for your customer. Package your product creatively, and include a personal note when you send it. These kinds of details will make you stand out in the minds of your customers — personal touches that will make people remember you and buy crafts from you again.

On the importance of community:

People who are involved with Teams on Etsy are more successful than those who aren't. Being an active member of your community is vital.

On the importance of making your online store stand out from the pack:

Take great photographs. Describe your products really well and in general-enough terms so that someone who is not an expert in your medium can understand what you're selling. I would also use your descriptions as a chance to tell your product's story. People love buying handmade, and your stories provide a deeper meaning for your customers.

Promotional Postcards

Postcards are not just for mailing from your vacation hotspot! There are so many ways you can utilize these handy, cost-effective rectangles.

I have quite a collection of lovely postcards that I've either received in the mail after purchasing things online or that I've picked up at craft fairs. I usually tack them up on a bulletin board or hang them on my inspiration wire. I also find them a great go-to source when I'm looking for a gift or want to rediscover work online.

Postcards can pack a big marketing punch with very little effort on your part. You can distribute them seasonally, when you introduce new products to your line, or when you have something special to promote. They make a great cross-promotional tool as well. Say you mostly sell your hand-thrown pottery, but you've decided to expand into tabletop items like coordinating coasters and placemats. Next time you're packing up a box of mugs or bowls, include a postcard showcasing your new wares; it may just result in another order.

Postcards are also an affordable way to send a bigger message than your business card has room for. Again, you need to make sure they contain all of your contact information and also fit in with your overall brand.

If you're concerned about making the investment in postcards, approach a pal whose work complements your own, and pay the cost together. Simply print your information on one side of the card and your friend's on the reverse. When you divvy up the postcards to hand out, you'll also be using the cards as a means of promoting each other's work to your individual client bases.

Business Name Tags and Stamps

If you're selling anything meant to be worn or carried — be it sewn, knit, crocheted, or any other medium — invest in tags with your business name on them. Wallets, iPod cozies, dresses, or scarves . . . whatever it is, identify your product with your business name. From shoes to cast-iron pots, manufacturers put their names on the products they sell for a reason. Take a page from their book and do the same. Nothing is more frustrating than admiring something and not knowing who made it and where it came from so that you can get one for yourself. Maybe that amazing knitted hat you mailed out to a customer last week was purchased as a birthday gift, and someone at the birthday party will desire one for herself. You want her to be able to examine the hat and know where to get a similar one — and to be able to tell the next person who admires it where they can get one, too.

Jewelry, of course, is a different matter; it's not possible to mark every piece with your business name. But you *can* mark the packaging they come in (stamp the box you send your handmade creations in with your company name or have a sticker made of your logo), or have little metal tags made to go on the clasps of bracelets and necklaces.

A stamp or stickers with your business name and logo can be used for all kinds of things and cost you very little. You can get them made at any big-box office supply store, or have one custom-made for you by an online company with an image you design and upload directly to their website. Make sure it fits in with your branding scheme, of course, and at least has your Web address on it. You can use your stamp or stickers to add a little something to the outside of your packaging, to stamp the back of receipts at craft fairs, to mark your shipping boxes, and lots more ways to identify your business.

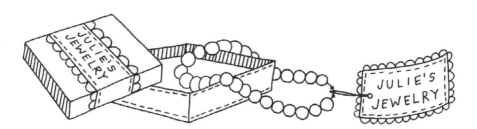

Photographs Are Key

A beautiful photograph is a tribute to the work you put into your craft. You need beautiful photographs for your store, your blog, and your marketing materials. How to get them? First of all, making your digital camera work for you isn't as hard as it may seem to be. With a combination of basic experimenting, some tools you already have in your house, and a bit of patience, you can learn to shoot lovely photos — the kind your products deserve. It also wouldn't hurt to learn basic photo editing, but you don't need to invest in anything horribly expensive.

Setting up a photography studio in your home can be a snap. All you basically need is a steady base, like a table, near a natural light source, like a window.

Take as many shots of your items as you can from all different angles. Once you download them to your computer and look at them up close, you may find a hidden gem or an angle that you never thought of before that will make your bar of handmade soap look incredible.

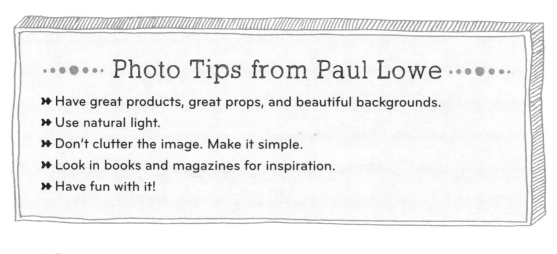

⋯⋯•⋯ Photo Tips from Paul Lowe ⋯•⋯⋯

➤➤ Have great products, great props, and beautiful backgrounds.
➤➤ Use natural light.
➤➤ Don't clutter the image. Make it simple.
➤➤ Look in books and magazines for inspiration.
➤➤ Have fun with it!

Setting Up a Light Box

Perhaps the best apparatus for photographing small- to medium-sized items is a light box, which is just a fancy name for a three-sided box that you can haul out when you're ready to have a photo shoot. It's easy to build (you probably have almost everything you need in your house right now to build one), and it's worth the time to do so.

Find a decent-sized box and remove one of the sides and the top, leaving three sides and a bottom. (A three-sided box lets you shoot from above or straight on.) A large packing box will do, even an old plastic storage tub will work. Heck, as long as it has three sides, just about anything will suffice. You'll also need some clean, unwrinkled white paper that's able to fit over all sides of the box and an adjustable lamp like a swing-arm desk lamp or even one of those clip-on silver industrial lamps that are available at any hardware store.

Now attach the white paper inside the box's three sides and bottom with bulldog or binder clips. Then set up your lamp, and shine it into the box. Place your item in the box, and adjust the light to your liking. There should be no glare on the object you're photographing. If you need to diffuse the light, try putting a piece of sheer fabric or even a dryer sheet over the light (making sure it won't catch fire!) or redirecting (reflecting) the light by bouncing it off a piece of white or black paper or even the ceiling. Okay, now you're ready to lean in and click away.

Use clean, wrinkle-free white paper as a background to help you achieve that floating-in-white-space look.

Propping Your Photos

As well as a writer, I'm lucky to be a freelance stylist, which allows me to justify buying pretty things if I think they'll come in handy during a photo shoot, even if I don't personally need them. Chances are, though, you already have all the props you need around the house to help your potential customers visualize how your crafts will look in their homes.

Pay attention to the next magazine you read, and note how secondary objects in a photo can enhance the main focal point. A simple vase of flowers or a lovely dishtowel in the background can make a photo come alive. If you make greeting cards, try shooting your newest thank-you note on a desk with a beautiful writing instrument nearby, or maybe dangle your latest handbag from a hook on a colored wall. The possibilities of improving your photographs with props are endless.

Photograph small items on a plain, solid background. Small things can get lost on fabric that's too busy or if there is too much else around them. Take close-ups of them in natural light. For larger items, try using scrapbook paper or wrapping paper or even some great fabric as your backdrop.

Try to have fun when you're working with your camera. Try new angles, different backgrounds and backdrops. As with your crafts, your own unique style will emerge, and soon you'll be just as comfortable with a camera in your hand as you are with, say, a paint brush.

••• Read the Manual! ••••

One of the best ways to become friends with your camera is to read the manual. That may also sound like one of the most boring ways to be friends with your camera, but it works. After all, who knows more about your camera, you or the camera manual? The manual explains what all of those symbols mean and how to change your settings. Some cameras allow you to easily adjust the white balance, which can result in crisper, clearer photos. Don't know what I'm talking about? Then you better get reading, my friend.

Karen Walrond of Chookooloonks

There is a lot of frustration out there when it comes to photographing of one's wares. I turned to Karen Walrond, an amazing photographer, to help me demystify this aspect of marketing for you.

I can't afford to buy a really expensive camera. Will my regular old point-and-shoot digital do when it comes to taking decent photos of my goods for the Web?

If it's a decent point-and-shoot, you can absolutely take great pictures of your goods. The beauty of single-lens-reflex cameras, or SLRs, is that you can switch out lenses, plus have more control over how your camera takes a photograph; however, today's point-and-shoots are also capable of taking amazing shots. The trick is to make sure that you're not taking the shots too closely to your subject [as to be blurry] or too far away [so that you can't discern any detail]; also, make sure that your subject is well lit. In general, a well-lit subject is the first big step in taking a great shot.

On the subject of "really expensive cameras," consider buying a secondhand camera. You can often get a really good secondhand SLR for the same price as a really good new point-and-shoot. I purchased my first SLR 15 years ago, and back then it was a 10-year-old camera body with 10-year-old lenses. I don't use the camera body anymore (I prefer digital), but I still use the lenses to this day. My only advice is to go to a reputable camera shop and actually try out the camera before you buy.

I have no idea what the settings on my camera mean. Is there a formula for taking a good picture?

Well, there are certain basic technical aspects of your camera that you should know to take a good picture. Probably the biggest one to be aware of is the ISO — this tells you how easily your camera will "catch light." The lower the number, the less your camera will have to "work" to catch light, so use a low number (100, 200, 400) in bright sunlight. The higher the number, the more your camera is working to "catch light" — a high number ISO (800, 1000, 1200) is good for dimmer light.

I've heard that flash isn't the way to go when taking photos of objects. Why? Wasn't the flash invented to help bring light to what I'm doing?

It *is* intended to bring light. The problem is that unless you're really good with a flash, the light looks unnatural. If you have a choice, shooting a subject with abundant ambient natural light is always nicer than shooting with a flash.

Speaking of light, when I try to "see" light, I just see, well, light. Could you explain that a little bit?

When you "see light," you're not just looking at the light but, more importantly, how the light is falling. Is it creating shadows? Is it dappled? Is it golden? White hot? Dim? Is it making your subject sparkle? Gleam? Is the light falling dully on a matte surface?

It is true that the trick to good photography is being able to see the light — and when you're really good, to *manipulate* the light. It just takes practice. So start by just noticing the light in your day-to-day life, separate from photographs: your favorite window or sun-dappled corner of your house, the bright midday sun and how it affects the way things or people look in its rays . . . . Once you've noticed the differences, grab your camera and start shooting it.

I've also heard it is not a good idea to photograph stuff outside. Why?

I *love* photographing things outside! Outdoor light often results in a much crisper, more detailed shot. Just be aware of:

- ▶ **Backgrounds.** If you're photographing a product, backgrounds can be distracting. Place your product on a really bland background or, alternately, create a "seamless background" — a large white piece of paper, for example. What photographers call no-seam paper is ideal.

- ▶ **Shadows.** Make sure that there aren't any strange shadows caused by the sun. Overcast skies can be a great way to shoot your product.

What are your basic tips for taking a really good picture? Are there any supplies other than a camera that I need to take photos?

No. Tripods or fancy flashes can be nice to have, but you don't need them. A good camera and some decent light, and you should be able to take a great shot.

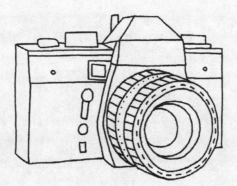

Chapter 5

YOUR CRAFT COMMUNITY

A new endeavor means exploring and putting yourself out there to make connections. If you start a new job, you network with your new coworkers and the people in your industry; if you relocate to a new town, you start exploring, and before you know it, you feel like you've always known some people, and you have lots of favorite places where you like to hang out. The same is true of starting a new business. It all comes down to community — especially the craft community.

Making Connections

Community. Your life wouldn't be the same without it. The people that ring you up at the grocery store, your friends and family and coworkers, all of these people make up your community. They are your champions — and they're also your best business leads in terms of spreading the word about you and your creations. They want to help and support you, and they are there for you. The same is true of your fellow crafters.

These days, you can join a crafting community anywhere in the world, thanks to the Internet. Social-media websites are popping up all the time, and all online marketplaces have forums that you can participate in. You can expand your community to include people you haven't even met but who can be there for you in lots of the same ways that your in-person local community is. Just sharing your crafts and your knowledge builds community. Asking questions, participating in online discussions, and engaging folks with your love of creating all build community.

Online Communities

Joining together with other crafters who have something in common with you is a great way to promote your work and market yourself. Being a part of and actively engaging in a crafting community (whether you call yourselves a team or a group of like-minded folks) will be invaluable to your business, and networking with these folks will truly benefit what you're doing. In fact, there is so much for you to do and so much you can share and learn that neglecting to get involved can hurt your business. You can exchange information about supplies, techniques, marketing tips, and more. Plus you'll be making new friends who share your interests. Becoming an active member in these kinds of communities can help you sell more plus enhance your crafting.

All the big online marketplaces have forums or message boards, and I strongly encourage you to interact with them. Perhaps you'll even discover a group in your city or town or region.

The most surprising challenge was fighting my baser instincts when becoming good friends with amazing artisans who are on the same path but already more successful than me. It's important to overcome the human inclination to feel jealousy and instead focus on one's inherent goodwill and joy for others' success.

— **LIZ SMITH**

If I knew then what I know now, I would have reached out to the community sooner instead of hoping someone would "find" me!

— **TARA SWIGER**

It was so sweet to see all the handmade gifts made by my crafter friends when my daughter Chloe was born. There's a real sense of sisterhood/brotherhood because we are all working together to invigorate the world with crafts!

— **NATALIE ZEE DRIEU**

I love connecting with other artists and crafters in person and online and feeling like I'm part of making the world a more beautiful place with my hands.

— **MATI ROSE MCDONOUGH**

Join Forces

You know that motto the Three Musketeers are famous for: "All for one and one for all." The same could be true of crafters. Joining forces can produce bigger, better results — that is, bigger, better sales. Look for what these days are popularly called "street teams"; this marketing term was originally used by indie record labels to describe a group of people who "hit the streets" to promote an event or a product. When you find an appropriate street team, join up. As crafters, you can join forces and make packets that include everyone's information or small samples of your work that each member of the team sends out when they mail a package to a customer. Personally, I love getting these packets in the mail. It exposes your work to people who might not have found you otherwise, and it's a great way to support your crafting community. And if you can't find a group like this — well, start your own.

But you say you make quilts, and obviously you can't send a sample quilt, so what good would a team do you? True enough, you can't send a quilt. But you *can* send tiny swatches that you've turned into magnets, or you can take pieces of the fabric you use to quilt and turn them into pushpins with a little flag with your business name. Do what you already do best: Be creative!

Community Swaps

One of my favorite things each winter is joining an online ornament swap. The swap I like is run by two women who post sign-ups on their blogs, and after the sign-up deadline has passed, they match me up with 10 other crafters whom I then swap with. I usually choose to swap with people from all over the world. I can honestly tell you that I look forward to this every year. My friends will often laugh at me

when, in the middle of summer, I'm plotting out what I'm going to make for my holiday ornament that year. But I've made new friends and contacts and garnered traffic to my blog and my Flickr account as a result of this swapping with strangers.

The particular swap I belong to asks participants to upload photos of what they make and what they received to a Flickr group devoted to that year's swap. A lively discussion goes on among the crafters who are swapping, and most people who do the swap have blogs (see chapter 6), where they post photos of what they get and usually include a link back to the maker's blog.

The creative benefits of participating in something like this are less obvious but no less invaluable. You can try new techniques and experiment with work on a smaller scale than perhaps what you're used to. Plus, of course, you get something in return. I love pulling out all the ornaments I've received during the years and displaying them around my home and office during the holiday season.

You can find swaps easily. Check the message boards on websites like Craftster, and find a swap that suits your desires. Fun is just around the corner!

FROM THE CREATIVE COLLECTIVE: **NICOLE VAUGHAN**

I think people can gain new crafty friends, a sense of participating in a global creative community, and a warm fuzziness by creating something for others and customizing it just for the recipient. [Swapping] can also be challenging and push you creatively.

XX XX XX XX XX XX XX XX XX XX XX XX X XX X XX XX X X XX XX XX X X XX XX XX X XX X XX XX XX XX XX XX XX XX XX Xx

Grace Bonney of Design*Sponge

Writer Grace Bonney launched Design*Sponge, a daily website dedicated to home and product design, in August 2004. The New York Times declared Design*Sponge the "Martha Stewart Living for the Millennials." The site includes store and product reviews, DIY projects, before-and-after furniture and home makeovers, trend forecasting, and recipes. In addition, Design*Sponge covers student design and national and international design shows. The site is updated not just daily but throughout the day, with an average of 6 to 10 posts a day, and has a huge core group of devoted readers.

What led you to create Design*Sponge?

A mixture of boredom and passion. I didn't see the sort of things I wanted to read about in magazines and wasn't being excited by the content I did see. But I had a real passion for design, so I decided to write about the things I liked online, instead. I never knew I would be doing this as a full-time job — I just sort of try to enjoy the ride and see where it goes.

To get coverage on Design*Sponge, what should people be sure to include to attract your attention?

Submissions e-mails are always best when they're two things: short and sweet. Politeness really can't be overstated. I always say your product should sell itself, so all you need to do is:

➤ Include good photos of your work, two to four of them in low-res JPEG form (no PDFs because you don't know if they'll work on everyone's computer).

81

- Include three short paragraphs: an intro about you and your work; details on why your work is different or innovative; and details on price, size, materials, and where you can buy it.

- Be sure to include the editor's name, spelled correctly (nothing says "I didn't try hard" like starting an e-mail with "To Whom It May Concern" or "Dear Editor").

If your work is a good fit, the pictures and basic info should be more than enough. Editors are happy to call back and get more personal information, but an initial contact e-mail shouldn't contain artist statements, personal biographies, or anything that isn't directly related to your product and its basic selling points. And please don't ever beg someone to write about your work because you had a death in the family, it's your birthday, or because you're "having a really bad year."

What information do you find helpful in a press kit, and what is your preferred method for receiving this kind of information?

I *only* accept electronic press kits. Aside from the ecological importance, I tend to work with and focus on independent designers whose budgets are tight and resources need to be efficiently doled out. I think samples should be sent only if required or specifically requested; why waste budget on sending samples to everyone? Instead, create a digital press kit that you can send to anyone — you can even create a free blog page where you host all your images and press releases. That way you can point people to all of your information with an easy URL link.

A lot of small companies are now handing out small flash drives as their official press kits. A flash drive is tiny, holds a ton of information and images, and doesn't lead to piles of printouts and paper. It's a great combination of ecofriendly and cost-efficient to make a simple online press kit to send to people.

I'd suggest including:

- A simple press release (this can be written in the form of a post or an "about" page on a company blog or site) about who you are.

- Great images of your work and any variations or options in your collection that can be shown visually.

- Information on purchasing and availability.

- Details on the work (size, materials, price).

- Info on what sets your work apart (is there an environmental story, a story about working with local artists, etc?).

You can even go so far as to upload podcasts or videos of your work process. These all allow an editor to connect more deeply to you without flowery press releases and long stories. Images are always the most powerful form of telling your story.

What makes you responsive to someone?

Normally it's the work alone. This is a visual industry, so I try to pay attention to the work first. If something is beautiful or grabs me for any given reason (whether it's a particular pattern or color or form), I'm intrigued and read on. If something doesn't grab me right away, I'll read on to see if there's something compelling about the piece I didn't see at first — but mostly it's a gut response to the actual visual work itself.

How do you decide what to feature on your website?

If a product does all of the things I mention above, and it hasn't already been covered online, I usually decide to post it. I like to focus on work that hasn't been covered before because I really try to offer my readers something new and fresh.

What best advice would you offer a crafter who is looking to gain national attention for their work?

Invest in great product photography. Great work sells itself, so you need to do everything possible to make sure the beauty of your work comes through in a way that's apparent to people reading about you online or in print because most people won't see your work in person.

With that done, create a simple digital press kit, and start from the ground up. Get coverage on blogs, local papers, or newsletters — all those things put you in front of bigger eyes, like those belonging to magazine editors, TV producers, or buyers. Once you build up some attention, pick your favorite magazine to give the first chance at a story.

Chapter 6

BLOGGING

Statement of fact: If you want to be in business, you need a Web presence. An online address — be it a blog or a website — is the easiest and most cost-effective way for you to market yourself. There is no other way that you can reach people from all around the world at all hours of the day and night without having to even be in attendance. Furthermore, this is the number-one way you can build community around your brand, build buzz about your work, and make money *while* you are eating your lunch, walking your dog, or even sleeping. Your online site is working for you 24/7. It will be your best employee, your most loyal fan, and the best business partner you can imagine.

Maintaining a blog or website can be a really rewarding experience. Not only will it help your business grow, you'll experience personal benefits as well, like making new friends and new contacts — and you'll learn a lot, too!

I'm going to make a crazy declaration here and say that I think a fantastic website or a well-run blog will wind up being the best tool you have when it comes to selling what you make. Your site will be as valuable to you as your glue gun, sewing machine, or crochet hook. Seriously.

Before we dig into the whys and wherefores of successful websites and blogs, I'd like to examine the differences between the two.

Blogs and Websites Defined

Although people sometimes use the words interchangeably, these two types of online sites are distinct variations on a theme.

A blog (short for *weblog* — and for the record, I have never heard *anyone* use the word "weblog") is a place on the World Wide Web where you set up camp and invite the entire world to pull up a chair and get to know you better. A blog is an online journal of what is going on with whatever your focus is. You can choose to focus on just your crafty endeavors or you can focus on personal stuff or you can mix it up and do both, like I do. A blog can have links to such things as your online store and a link to your Flickr account, but generally you do not have a shopping cart set up in a blog. You use the blog to inform your audience about what you're doing and to direct them to other places where they can find you on the Internet.

A website is a bit broader. It can *include* a blog, but generally speaking, the primary point of a crafter's website is to sell product. It probably has a shopping cart built into it so that people can buy your goods directly from your website without leaving the site to travel to another source to make purchases.

So there you have it. Both blogs and websites can have the same features, like an about page, a press page, and a FAQ (Frequently Asked

Questions) page. But one would likely have a built-in shopping cart, and one's main focus is to offer an informative peek into your personal or business life or both!

Basic Setup

If you decide to go with a website, a couple of things should be considered. For starters, unless you are good with HTML and CSS, you may need to hire a web designer to get your website the way you want it. And even if you hire a designer, you will most likely need to learn some basic code so that you can make changes and updates when you want to. Then you need to find a hosting company you like and make sure the name you choose is available.

Make sure you have some money available, too, because websites don't always come cheap. The hosting will generally cost money and so will registering a dot-com — not to mention that designers can charge either by the hour or by the project, and their time can add up.

That being said, having a well-designed website can make you look more professional, especially to retail outlets that you may want to wholesale your goods to. Your audience won't expect you to update your website as often as a blog, and once you learn how to make changes on your own, your duties to your website can be minimal.

However, if you want to start small and test out the whole commitment to having an online presence, a blog

FROM THE CREATIVE COLLECTIVE: **NICOLE VAUGHAN**

I've met people all over the world online through my crafting blog and made great friends who just "get" why I'd be excited about a piece of fabric or a ball of yarn.

is the way to go. First of all, there are *many* free options out there. Simply find a blogging website you like, sign up, choose a template, and be blogging by the time it would normally take you to eat breakfast. With a blog, you can easily hold off on the whole designer thing if you want to, and most blogging platforms will allow you to add pages so that you can incorporate additional layers to your blog, like the "about me" and press pages I mentioned earlier. You can tell what blogging service your favorite blog authors are using by name (preceded by a period, or dot) at the end of their Web address. Some pretty common ones are .blogspot, .typepad, and .wordpress.

No matter what platform you choose to go with, having a blog element is pretty important. You probably read blogs and have some favorites. (And if you don't read any blogs, you should! Check out the blogs and websites of the Creative Collective in the Resources section at the back of this book for some great places to start.)

Writing a Successful Blog

Loads of creative people feel that their talents, while vast and varied, end when it comes to writing. If that's you, fear not! Writing posts for your blog doesn't have to be scary or hard. Just remember that your blog is all about whatever you want it to be about.

······ Best Reasons to Blog ······

➤➤ Receive valuable feedback from your customers and your community.

➤➤ Garner support for projects you're working on.

➤➤ Keep customers updated on what's new.

➤➤ Make new friends and grow your community.

You can write as little or as much as you want, when you want, and, most importantly, about whatever you want.

Because you are human, some personal stuff is bound to sneak in despite your best intention to keep it strictly professional (if that is your goal). Maybe you'll want to post an adorable photo of your puppy sitting on the sofa next to some pillows you made, or give a sneak peak of an anniversary card you're making for your husband. Pretty much no matter what — even if you're very, very careful — your blog will not only be about what you sell but about who you are as well. Stay true to yourself when you're posting, and you'll be fine no matter how you personally feel about your own writing. People will enjoy getting to know you better, and they'll appreciate a behind-the-scenes look at the life of someone whose work they admire.

Finding Your Voice

What does "voice" mean, anyhow? It means style. Just as you found your crafting style, you'll soon find your writing style after a little practice. Just stay true to how you talk in real life, and you'll do fine. Are you jokey and funny when you're hanging out with your friends talking about your creative side? Let that shine through in your writing. Are you into details

FROM THE CREATIVE COLLECTIVE: LIZ SMITH

I love to write. I love sharing information. I love posting pretty pictures. And I love hearing how my posts have been helpful, inspiring, amusing, et cetera. I think people enjoy knowing about the person behind the craft, and I like providing that information.

X X X X X X X X X X X X X X X X X X X X X X X X X X X X X X X X X X X X X X X X X X X X X X X X X X X X

Three Rules for Blogging Success from Grace Bonney of Design*Sponge

1. Focus on what makes you YOU. If you have a background in a certain field or live in an interesting area of the world that hasn't been covered a lot, focus on those things. Blogs that are about interesting fields always stand out from the pack.

2. Keep things simple — it's always better to have fewer posts and content if those fewer things are original and thought-provoking.

3. Focus on the editorial content. Sure, ad revenue can be nice, but it shouldn't be the focus of a site. Focus on what you love and write about that; the rest can potentially grow from there.

and teaching others? If so, *that* should come out in your writing.

Just imagine your blog posts as a one-sided conversation with a friend about a topic you're passionate about, and that fervent, friendly tone will trickle out your fingers, through your keyboard, and into your writing, creating a blog destined to be a big hit in the blogosphere.

What's the Look of Your Blog?

Does your blog's appearance reflect your working style? If not, work on that. Your blog is a part of your branding, and it should reflect what your business is all about. Even if you chose a free template when you signed up for your blog, there are ways to customize it. Make the banner reflective of *you*. Change up the side-bars, and make sure you have a Flickr badge or a link that leads people to your online store. Change the background colors seasonally or to match your current line. There are lots of ways to make this resource your own, and it isn't as hard to do as it may sound at first.

Again, if you find yourself having trouble with this part of your blog, you'll be able to find many creative businesspeople to help you out. A quick search on websites like Etsy pulls up numerous resources for folks who design banners (those headers across the top of the page) or skins (decorative backgrounds that are easily changed) for blogs. Poke around your favorite blogs, and make a list of what you like and what you don't like about what you see. This is a great way to get some inspiration when you're trying to determine what you'd like for your own blog.

In search of a designer who can help you build your website from top to bottom? Check websites you admire, and see if you can ascertain who designed the website. Usually you'll find credits somewhere, most likely on the bottom of the first page of the website.

If you go with a designer, you'll need to have a clear idea from the get-go of what you want for yourself. I have almost always worked with a designer for my own blogs, and each time I've had work done on a site I've owned, I needed to give detailed examples of what I wanted, sometimes even having to draw pictures of my ideal site if I couldn't find anything similar to show my designer.

Common Blog and Website Terms

BLOG READER OR FEED READER
A website that collects the updated information from all of the websites you subscribe to. These are free services, and two of the most popular ones are www.beta.bloglines.com and www.reader.google.com.

CSS
CSS stands for Cascading Style Sheets, which is the computer language used by website designers that controls how sites look.

CATEGORIES
Categories are tags that people use to file their online postings. Usually they are searchable terms on a website. For example, if you posted about shoes, yarn, and cherry pie, your categories might be fashion, yarn, and desserts. Your readers may want to search your blog or website for entries that cover a specific topic, and using category tags are very helpful.

DASHBOARD
This is the control panel your blogging platform uses. It is where you actually write your posts or upload photos.

HTML
Short for HyperText Markup Language. This is a computer language used to format a Web page (think boldfacing or italicizing or creating paragraphs) as well as for inserting hyperlinks and images. Most Web platforms have tools built into their dashboards that add basic HTML for you.

RSS FEED
RSS stands for Real Simple Syndication. Most websites, blogs, and even online shops have a RSS symbol, usually some sort of orange icon, that allows you to subscribe to the site, sending all updates to the feed reader or news aggregator service of your choice.

SEO
Stands for Search Engine Optimization. People use SEO strategies to increase traffic to their websites by using key words that make them easier to find and rank in search engines.

STATISTICS
These can be useful for tracking who is coming to your site, linking to you, and what search words they use to find you.

How Often Should You Post?

Deciding how often to post on your blog can be a tough question to answer. Basically you should post as often as is comfortable for you. If writing is new to you, and you feel a little unsure of yourself, you might prefer posting once a week. If you're more at ease with the process, post daily.

Take note of the blogs you enjoy the most. How often are *those* blog authors posting? Try using one of your favorite blogs as a guide, and match them post for post as a sort of exercise. You should consider your readers, though. People tend to check in more often if you post more often.

You can sign up for many free Internet services that will help you track the traffic to your blog. In turn, you can use these facts to figure out how to improve your blog.

You may find that most people read your site on Fridays but almost no one checks in on Mondays, so you might want to adjust the specific days you're posting. Or you could discover that someone you didn't even know was linking to your site, and once you see all the traffic flowing in from them, you'll want to check them out. You will also be able to tell what random Internet searches bring people to your blog or certain key words that are bringing people back to it again and again.

No matter how often you decide to post, consistency is key. Your readers will come to know your pattern, and if you drop off the face of the blogosphere, they might drop you off of their blogs-to-read list. At a minimum, try to post at least once a week.

If you're going to be away from your blog for a long time — say, off on a vacation — you should let readers know before you disappear.

What Should You Post About?

Good blog content takes work. It can be tough to sit down in front of your computer every day, or even once or twice a week, and think of something interesting to write. First-rate content is much more involved than just throwing any old thing up on your site. Your posts don't have to be long or incredibly detailed — they just need to be stimulating and thoughtful. In fact, many people seem to enjoy shorter blog posts filled with good photographs. Readers generally subscribe to lots of blogs, and keeping up with all the posts can be overwhelming to some.

As time goes by and you learn what your readers respond to, finding ideas for your posts will become easier. Remember that little notebook I advised you, back at the beginning of this book, to have with you at all times? It will come in handy with your blogging. Every time you get an idea or have a great thought about something that would make good blog fodder, *write it down.* I can't tell you how many times I personally have sat down with the thought of blogging weighing heavily on my mind and wished I could remember that great idea I'd had earlier in the day.

When I asked my Creative Collective what they enjoyed most on their favorite blogs, I got the same replies again and again. People like to see great photos, funny writing, and, yes, even hear about your struggles. For example, if you're trying to find more outlets to consign your quilts,

FROM THE CREATIVE COLLECTIVE: **TARA SWIGER**

I blog to inform and to connect. I inform my customers about the benefits of a certain fiber, and I inform other artists by writing and sharing videos about specific spinning or dyeing techniques. I connect with the community by putting my ideas out there and asking for their ideas in return. It's a great back and forth, which helps feed the ideas!

the community will benefit from hearing how you approach stores and what challenges you're going through. Pretty much anything that connects your readers with your products will help you sell more.

EXPLAIN YOUR CREATIVE PROCESS

Without giving away any trade secrets, you can post a bit about your artistic process. Do you use your sewing machine in a cool way that you can share? Or do you organize your paintbrushes in an unusual fashion?

Any sort of behind-the-scenes peek into your craft that you can give your audience will be enjoyed.

TELL THE PERSONAL STORY BEHIND YOUR WORK

Write about why you do what you do. People love that. Do you make woodcut woodland animals because the best vacation you ever took was in a wonderful forest in Germany? Write about it. Maybe your grandmother taught you to knit. Write about your memories of that. As the expression goes, write what you know.

FROM THE CREATIVE COLLECTIVE: NATALIE ZEE DRIEU

A good tutorial has to have the perfect mix of visuals with instructions. That may be steps of photos with clear, concise directions or a video with voiceover. It's important also to focus on areas that you think may be complex for someone to understand. For instance, maybe you've uncovered a special technique to cast on for knitting. If it's hard to explain in instructions, having multiple photos and close-up shots always helps. Like they say, a picture is worth a thousand words.

OFFER IDEAS FOR WHAT TO DO WITH YOUR PRODUCTS

Do you make wristlets? Take photos showing people how to dress them up or dress them down. Perhaps you make coffee mugs. If so, you could offer up a hot-drink recipe every Friday to keep readers checking back in.

POST TUTORIALS

Are you an expert at what you make? Then share your knowledge. If you're skilled at making bath bombs, let people know what they should look for when buying them. Educating your customers is always a good idea. Every once in a while consider posting a tutorial. Whether the topic is a great dessert you made last weekend or a certain stitch you enjoy, people love to learn new things, and your blog is a great way to teach folks a new trick.

HOST CONTESTS AND GIVEAWAYS

A great way to get your name and your wares into the public eye is to host a contest and give something away on your blog or website! You could think up some trivia questions that relate to your art form or craft, and ask people to leave their answers in the comment section. You could give away some of your extra supplies, a PDF pattern, or even a one-of-a-kind creation of yours.

When I polled members of the Creative Collective, the one element everyone agreed makes them want to return often to certain blogs is good photographs. Bone up on the section about taking good photos — and invest in a decent camera if need be — to keep your readers interested.

Promote Your Blog Everywhere You Go

Promoting your blog is essential to its success. Some tips:

- ➤➤ When you engage in an online forum, be sure to leave your contact information so that people can see what you're all about.

- ➤➤ Make sure your Web address is on all of your marketing materials so that people can look you up. Don't overlook your sales receipts, your business cards, or even your shipping labels.

- Make sure your blog address is on all of your contact information such as your e-mail signature and any online profiles you may have.

- When posting, link to other websites and blogs that may complement what you're posting about. Helping to drive traffic to other blogs may help you get others to link to you.

- If you see something you like on someone else's blog and it inspires you to post about something similar, let the other blog author know! Leave a comment on their site informing them that you're linking back to their post.

Give and Take

Once you've created your blog, how will you get people to visit it and interact with you? Much like almost everything else in life, you'll get out of your online community what you put into it. When it comes to building traffic for your blog, the number-one way you can get people to notice you is to notice *them*. Leave thoughtful and valuable comments on blogs that have something in common with your own.

You'll need to learn the difference between leaving what is considered a spam type of comment and a genuine, thoughtful remark. When leaving comments for others, your goal is to add to and enhance the conversation going on within their comments section. Just reading someone's post, saying, "Pretty blog! Nice post!" and then leaving a link to your own blog doesn't really contribute to the conversation. Besides, others reading the comments will feel like you have nothing of value to chip in, giving them no incentive to click on the link back to *your* blog. It's important to interact with your readers. We all like to be acknowledged, so ask questions of your readers. They can leave their answers, and you can respond. If you're hoping to start a conversation with people, you need to be sure to participate back.

When you visit the blogs you like, leave a comment with your information for people to link back to. Join in their conversation or forum, and maybe they'll pay *your* blog a visit.

Managing Blog Comments

Comments can be nerve-racking. You can get loads of them and have a hard time keeping up, or you can get hardly any and wonder why. To avoid getting certain kinds of comments, some people start out with a comment policy in place. Usually your blogging software will have an option in your dashboard that will allow you to have control over what kinds of things people can post on your blog.

You can set up your comments to be held in your e-mail until you approve them. That way you can stop spam from getting in and keep "trolls" out. Many blog websites also offer CAPTCHA (the acronym for "Completely Automated Public Turing Test to Tell Computers and Humans Apart"). This option — which you've seen many times, even if you didn't know what they were called — is what you see when you log into a secure website or want to leave a comment somewhere, but first you have to type a nonsense word that is all squiggly and hard to read into a box.

You can encourage people to interact with you by asking them questions and inviting them to join

••• Tips for Posting Blog Comments •••

➡ Be thoughtful. Show them and the other readers that you read what the author had to say.

➡ Make sure your comment is relevant to the topic's post.

➡ Leave comments on blogs that have something in common with you, because your mutual readers will have something in common with one another. You likely wouldn't get any new readers to your "Jewelry Designing with Sarah" blog if you're leaving comments on the "Tricked-Out Tire Rims" blog.

in the conversation you've started. If you're writing about crafting supplies, ask people what their favorites are. Or if you're artistically stuck in a project, ask your readers for advice. Offering up the floor, as it were, is a great way to get readers involved, thereby making them more interested in you and your goods.

Respond to the comments your readers leave. Imagine how thrilled you'd feel if you were to leave a comment on the site of a crafter whom you admire, and they replied back! You have the power to make someone else feel just as special by responding in kind to their words.

Not getting many comments? Don't get upset or take it personally. Sometimes writing a blog can seem like a personality or popularity contest, and you may feel that you're just not measuring up. That's simply not true. Your main goal should be to connect with your customers, not worry about how many people check in on your every post. The people who buy and appreciate your work will be there for you — and they are who really count. Seriously, it's about getting the right people to read. That's what you're looking for.

With most blogging services, you can choose to have your comments on or off. If you're trying to actively engage your readers, you should leave them on.

What Makes a Blog Successful

Let's sum up what will make your blog attract readers — not just once but repeatedly.

- ❯❯ Have a clean-looking yet visually interesting site.

- ❯❯ Post as often as possible.

- ❯❯ Keep your content friendly, helpful, interesting, original (no cribbing from other bloggers!), and to the point (in both focus and length).

- ❯❯ PHOTOS, PHOTOS, PHOTOS — of you, your work, your dog and cat, your garden, your workbench; readers want to know who you are.

- Let your personality shine through in your writing voice.
- Offer free tutorials, archiving old ones and highlighting a new one.
- Provide links to like-minded and inspiring sites.

Create an Online Newsletter

You have a sign-up sheet at your table when you work craft booths, and you save all of your customers' e-mail addresses, right? So how are you going to use all of those addresses now that you've collected them? Why, you're going to write a newsletter. Not just any newsletter, though — a wonderful, amazing, information-filled, useful newsletter!

Newsletter, you say?! What in the world do you need to write a newsletter for? Who will read it? What good will it do you?

Well, for starters, if you are opposed to the idea of a blog, and you've decided to go with a website that you don't have to update all that often, a newsletter is a really good option for you to reach out to people a bit more. You can use a newsletter to amp up your marketing efforts by sending your customers and the craft community current info about what's going on with your business. (And don't fret about frequency; newsletters don't have to be weekly or monthly. They can be quarterly or even just seasonally.)

Chances are you get a newsletter mailed to your inbox every now and then from a business you've ordered from in the past, right? Maybe you purchased some shoes from them, and now once a week you get an offer for free shipping or an alert that new shoes in your size just came in. Companies send you these e-mails because they work.

I'm not suggesting that you spam your customers or send people electronic newsletters that they don't want. But if your audience is open to it, and you've given people the choice, by all means you should send them a newsletter.

Not surprisingly, the Creative Collective is big on blogging — their own and others' blogs. Here are some of their thoughts on the concept.

I love a blogger who's personal and isn't afraid to give opinions. I love when someone's voice is so clear and strong that you feel like you know them. I have a hard time connecting to blogs that aren't run by individuals or a group of individuals with strong personalities.

— GRACE BONNEY

I blog like crazy! It's a place to show and tell, ask for help, connect with other people, and pretend I have my own magazine with complete editorial control, which I absolutely love. I don't think I would have a business if it weren't for my blog. Most people enjoy supporting people they have a connection with — I know that's true for me. So if you dig what I do, you can visit me on my blog, not just buy my books. It's a great way to just put what you do out there with a more personal voice than just "buy my stuff."

— AMY KAROL

I love hearing what people think of my work. It has been a great opportunity to cultivate a community of like-minded artists and crafters. Our blogs are a sort of around-the-world conversation. I get excited when I realize an artist I admire has a blog, and I find it thrilling to have a glimpse into their process and workspace as well as into their thought pattern and inspiration sources, and I hope I can do that for others as well.

— LAURIE COYLE

We are each so diverse, yet the web can often flatten us, giving blogs a certain sameness, offering an insufficient variety. We as blog authors have the exciting challenge to transform the static into something animated, personal, and real. Consistent, creative, authentic, and honest viewpoints give a blog individuality, transforming a pretty page with text into something relevant and meaningful.

— HOLLY BECKER

Painting led me to start a blog, which then inspired me to create an artist website and then to open an Etsy shop, which in turn connected me to many gallery shows and the opportunity to sell my artwork in shops around the country! From there, opportunities that I could never have dreamed of appeared. It has been a very organic process that continues to unfold.

— MATI ROSE MCDONOUGH

Put Your Newsletter to Work

Your newsletter can do more than just keep people apprised of what's new — although it can certainly do that. A newsletter can also be used to:

- Let people know what's going on in your personal world of craft.
- Introduce new products or designs you've come up with.
- Let people know about your craft-show schedule.
- Offer giveaways, freebies, and other promotions.
- Offer specials or deals to preferred customers.
- Pass along any recent press you've received.

You can also invite your customers to be a part of your newsletter. Create a customer gallery, and ask people who have bought items from you to submit photos of them wearing your custom-made dresses or serving a salad on a platter you handcrafted.

A newsletter can also be called an e-mail blast or an e-mail alert. Basically an electronic newsletter is a fancy, pretty e-mail.

FROM THE CREATIVE COLLECTIVE: **TARA SWIGER**

I love my newsletter! It's fun to write, and it helps past customers (who might not read my blog) keep up with what's going on with my business. I find that I get a healthy spike in sales right after sending the newsletter and always hear from repeat customers. It works best when I use it to really connect with the customers, especially when I ask for their input on ideas.

Consider posting free downloads in your newsletter. Or offer tutorials! The possibilities are endless, and as long as you have willing readers, a newsletter is a fine way to keep in touch as an option to writing a blog.

Generating a Newsletter

Plenty of newsletter services are available on the Internet. Do a quick Google search, or ask around in your favorite online forum. Perhaps you already know someone who uses a newsletter service, and they can recommend one to you.

A service is going to help you do the tough stuff. Most of them have

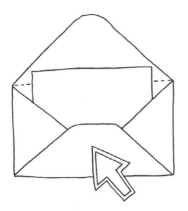

HTML built right into them, so it will be a snap to make the look of the newsletter consistent with your brand. You will easily be able to add photos, add links to your website or store, and a whole lot more.

It is really important that you respect people's privacy and ask their permission before you sign them up for your newsletter. But if you have a mailing-list sign-up sheet, people will expect to get mail, so you're covered. You can alert people who buy things from your online store that once they order from you, they will automatically be added to your newsletter list; just make sure you state it clearly in your shop policies or the about you section. But if someone wants to unsubscribe, remove them immediately, no questions asked. (The newsletter services also easily allow people to unsubscribe from as well as subscribe to your newsletter if they so choose.)

You can post a widget on your blog or website alerting folks to the fact that you have a newsletter, and they can sign up if they're interested.

Casey and Jessica from Ravelry

In 2007 Jessica Marshall Forbes had an idea for a website about knitting. She had been an avid knitter for some time and saw something lacking in the online community when it came to her hobby. Luckily her husband, Casey, a self-proclaimed computer addict, was able to realize the computer side of her vision, and together they created Ravelry. They took a love of crafting in a different kind of direction and created a crafty business that is very successful.

There is a strong sense of community on Ravelry. How did the two of you grow that?

When we started, we were small, and we put a lot of effort into helping to create the atmosphere that we wanted by participating *a lot*. We spent a lot of time in the forums and communicating with people on a one-on-one basis. We still do, but not like we used to. Ravelry is much bigger today than when we started, and there are tens of thousands of people who may not even know who the two of us are. Still, I think that the small beginning was an important formative time, and although the community as a whole is more likely to shape the site today than we are, the influence that the beginning "culture" had on the site can still be seen.

What are the benefits to joining online crafting communities?

People appreciate community for so many reasons, but mostly they make friends, have fun, and find support (whether in their hobby or in life) and make lots of real-life connections that they would have missed out on entirely.

Any tips that might be good for making friends online?

Share. It's amazing what the smallest detail about your interests or your life can lead to. Making friends online is a lot like real life in this regard; connections with people start small and simple: a common interest, a common struggle, an obscure detail that makes you realize that you have a connection with another person.

What is the best thing about owning your own business?

Being able to work on something that you care about, something that interests and excites you. Ravelry is even better because of the people. Not only is the work interesting and fun, but it is so rewarding to be making something for people who really appreciate it and are really interested and excited about making it better.

What is the worst thing about owning your own business?

The worst thing about owning your own business is the flip side of the best thing. When you really care, it's hard to separate work from the rest of your life. You can't easily punch out at the end of the day or the end of the week and forget about work until you return.

Moving [the business] out of our home was one of the best things that we did. We had no life when we worked at home — there was no separation at all between work and home life. We're so much happier now; the move has helped us have a healthier life in general.

By most standards, your business has grown very quickly. Did you turn to any professionals for help?

We've had two kinds of help: friends who are experts in their fields who are willing to talk and share advice (a friend helped us figure out our advertising plan, for example), and the sorts of professional services that every business needs. We didn't need a payroll company, a bookkeeper, and a lawyer right away, but we hired them when it was time.

Your business is not the typical crafty business, yet you saw a need and filled it. What advice do you have for other crafty people that might help them think outside the box when it comes to creating a business?

Actually, you said exactly what we would advise! If you see that there is a need for something and you think you could do a good job fulfilling it — go for it.

I don't know if we did everything right as we have gone along, but I do feel that growing slowly and starting out small has helped us. Starting small can make it easier for you to take the risk of getting started, which can be the scariest part!

I also think that the craft community online can be an enormous help. We found contacts in our industry, used them as a marketing tool, and found others who helped support us as we grew. Talk to people you trust about your business idea. Get samples out to people! Have them talk about your products on their websites! Team up with other craft businesses to see how you can help each other grow!

In the beginning, how many days a week and hours in a day were you working? Has that lessened any now?

After we both went full-time on Ravelry, we worked from morning until night for months. Even after Ravelry felt like it was rolling along and we could work a more normal schedule, it took a while for us to stop pouring all of our energy into it and take breaks. Now we work a more normal week — maybe 50 or 60 hours a week. And we take weekends off.

Chapter 7

ADVERTISING AND PUBLICITY

Advertising can mean much more than just placing a photo of your work and your name on a page in a newspaper or magazine. Think outside the ribbon box, and you'll find lots of unconventional ways to raise awareness of what you make, and reach far more potential customers than you ever imagined was possible!

Advertising Online

Online advertising might make as much sense for your business as traditional (that is, print) sources, if not more. Where do you hang out on the Web? Blogs that cover knitting? Design and decorating websites? Chances are most of those places host ads. Maybe you've even clicked on some of those ads yourself. They work, right? Check the advertising page of your favorite Web hangouts and see what their rates are. If the rates aren't listed (and they usually aren't), send an e-mail to the editor of the website, explain why you think your business is a good match for them, and ask what their rates are.

You may see that rates depend on whether or not you pay for an ad "ATF" or "BTF." Those acronyms mean *above the fold* and *below the fold*; anything on a computer screen that is visible without the viewer scrolling down is considered above the fold, whereas if you have to scroll down to read something, it is below the fold. These are newspaper terms going back to the idea that it's better if a story is printed on the upper half of a "broadsheet" (think the *New York Times*) to be visible when the paper is folded — above the fold. In today's online world, however, the likelihood is that people are going to scroll down a website no matter what. If, for example, a blogger posts more than once a day, a reader would most likely have to scroll down just to read that day's post in its entirety.

Often you can also buy ad space that is inserted between postings. Sometimes when you buy an ad, you will also get a highlighted post about you from the blog editor. Different blogs offer different choices for how long your ad will run. Make sure you know what you're getting into, and be sure you're comfortable with what the terms are. If you have questions about your contract, *ask*. Some blogs offer specials at different times of the year, and some offer deals to certain people such as artisans just starting out or women designers and so on.

Ads on blogs around holiday times are especially coveted, so be sure that you're informed as to when your favorite blogs or websites are taking ads for the season. You'll find that some sites require you to commit to an ad three months ahead of time, and you will most likely need to pay in full before your ad runs.

Podcasts

Another cost-effective advertising medium is sponsoring podcasts. Podcasts are a newer way to reach out to customers, and their impact on the creative community shouldn't be overlooked. These days lots of fantastic podcasts cover the handmade movement, and lots of them need show sponsors, which means they are seeking advertisers. A promotional

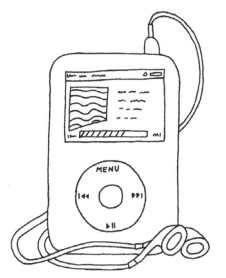

statement is usually read by the host of the podcast at the beginning and/ or end of their show. Ask them if they will also link to your store or website in their show notes or on their podcast's website besides reading your ad. For more about podcasts and podcasting, see chapter 8.

Join a Collective

Consider advertising with a collective: a group of people who get together to split the cost for a similar purpose. Various message boards and other crafty community websites aimed at artisans often have an advertising thread. Check them out, and see if any of the people putting together an ad collective are right for you. Make sure your work fits in with the group and that the proposed publication for the ad is a good match for your customer base. Generally, each of you submits a photo of your work and some basic information, like your business name, and then a group ad is designed around the pics and info. A collective ad is a great way to get a photo of what you make in a major publication that may otherwise be beyond your ad budget.

Use E-mail Signatures and Avatars

Do you have an e-mail signature? If not, you should! All e-mail programs that I know of allow people to create a standard e-mail signature that automatically gets included with every message you send. This simple addition turns all the electronic communicating you do into valuable advertising opportunities. Maybe you're sending an e-mail to your bank manager — and it just so happens that the bank hosts local artists in their lobby, and you're invited to be included. Or maybe you're sending an RSVP to a friend's sister-in-law who is hosting a baby shower you've been invited to, and she may be looking for baby gifts, which you happen to make. No matter whom you're writing to, including a link to your shop and website and your tag line are indispensable marketing tools. Your signature doesn't have to be very complicated or professionally designed. Just the facts will do.

Likewise, when you comment on websites or blogs, have a signature ready to go that you can just plug in at the end of your comment. This one may be a bit simpler than your e-mail signature, but it should still contain your basic information.

Lots of places online also have the capability for you to include an avatar for your signature (see chapter 8 to learn about avatars). Basically, you need to decide if you want to have a photo of yourself or a photo of what you create. If you have a business logo, the choice of what to include is already made for you.

Message Boards and Forums

Message boards are a great place to spread the word about what you're selling and also a great place to consider advertising. Who are your primary customers? Working mothers? Hipsters? Teenagers? Chances are there are community forums where these people hang out online. Find those places, and then figure out how to fit yourself and your work into the conversation to let them know about you and how to find your product. Consider asking these audiences for advice when designing a new product. These places are also excellent for finding people to beta test what you're making if you need that kind of support and feedback. If you end up connecting with a new customer this way, you may be able to score some wonderful testimonials that you can use on your website or an awesome quote you can plug into a media alert or press release.

Check and see if these sites have rules about postings before you go hog wild pushing your products. Many of them try to keep advertising spam out of their communities, and you might possibly turn people off just as easily as you can turn them on. Make sure you can be a valuable contributor and that you and your wares are a good match for the site. Even if you

just chime in with practical advice or support, having your information in your signature line can be helpful to your business.

Make the Most of Your Blog and Website

You have friends on the Internet. Like-minded crafters whose work you enjoy and support are the people who enjoy and support your work in turn. These folks are your community, and you need to help each other grow and expand. When it comes to creative advertising, Internet friends are a wonderful cost-effective resource.

As you have probably noticed from spending time on blogs in general, whether or not they are related to your handmade passions, they usually have a designated place where other websites or blogs they like are listed. Sometimes links are "swapped," as in "if you link to me, I'll link to you"; sometimes people just link to sites they personally love, even if they have no other connection.

Make sure that you are linking to other blogs and Web shops that have a well-matched audience. Write to the owners of these blogs and offer a link exchange, but don't stop with just your Web address. Investigate making banners or badges or blinking buttons — whatever appeals to you — and offer to swap with other sites you like. As long as you know the size dimensions the other website can handle, you can make your own standout ad that will lead people from other websites back to you and your product.

Don't think you have the skills to make a flashing badge yourself? Not to worry. Lots of creative people out there will do it for you. A simple search for badges or banners on the many online craft marketplaces will turn up affordable services, and you can hire another creative person to make a custom ad just for you.

COMMENTING ON OTHER BLOGS AND WEBSITES

Leaving comments on websites can be intimidating sometimes, I know. But if a design blog editor recently did a big roundup of beautiful handmade chairs, and you create chair cushions, this is a good time to take off your shy shoes and leave a great comment. Perhaps you have some inside industry commentary you can provide, or maybe you just want to compliment the chairs. No matter, figure out something nonspammy and clever to say, make sure you work your cushions into the comment, and make doubly sure your contact information has been left behind.

It goes without saying, but I'm going to do so anyway: you should *never* spam a blog or website with your advertising information. However, when you leave a comment on an online post, make sure your signature line is included, and that can usually include a link back to your store or website.

Be Your Own Best Ad Agency

Create your own advertising. Make up flyers, or have a beautiful postcard printed, featuring your work and your information. Put them up wherever your customers are likely to be. Most coffee shops, art stores, and some cafés have bulletin boards where people can hang things for free. Post your work! Beyond that, some other advertising options can enhance your exposure, and they won't cost you a cent (or maybe only a few cents).

Be a Walking Advertisement

Wearing or using what you make is also a great way to advertise. When someone compliments you on your fabulous skirt or your gorgeous hand-knit scarf, tell them you made it — and they can own one just like it. Then hand them your business card (which, of course, you will have with you at all times). Seeing your work in use is a great way to sell it and generate buzz.

Another option is to trade your products. Do you have a crafty friend who makes something that appeals to the same market as your goods? If your friend makes fantastic head-bands, say, and you make great hats,

⋯⋯ True Story ⋯⋯

A company I personally love and have ordered from again and again is Queen Bee Creations in Portland, Oregon. This company makes beautifully crafted vegan bags, wallets, hip pouches, cases, diaper bags, and more. They offer an option to request extra business cards be sent with an order. These cards are meant for satisfied customers to pass out each time someone asks them about their Queen Bee products. I can honestly tell you that I have given away every extra card they have ever sent to me. This simple low-cost method on Queen Bee's part has allowed this customer to easily and effectively spread the word about their products all across the country and in one case across the Atlantic: I was in an airport in France, and the airline counter person asked me where I got my wallet. I was able to whip out Queen Bee's business card and pass it along. Word-of-mouth advertising should not be overlooked or minimized.

trade items. When you have the chance to talk up her headband, do so, and give out her business information — and she'll do the same for you.

Donate Your Wares

Watch the newspapers and other news outlets in your town for announcements of art-based fundraisers. Often these are annual events, and organizers rely on people to donate goods and services to raise money, usually through silent auctions. Find a charity that fits in with your audience, and consider donating something to their cause. Don't think about it as giving away your product; think about it as reaching an untapped sector of your target audience. Plus, of course, you'll be supporting your community.

As people browse the silent auction, they will have the chance to examine your craft up close and personal before they bid on it. And if they don't win what you donated or if they want additional pieces, your contact information will be available for them to find you. Perhaps you'll get to attend the event yourself as well. In any event, your business name should be listed in the program or on the charity's website.

Your donation is tax deductible for the value of the item, so make sure you get a receipt from the charity, and save it for tax time.

Exercises in Creative Marketing

Think about what you craft. Now try to think of new ways you can get your message across to people about your wares without giving away a full sample of your product. I'm a big fan of handing out useful things. Thumbtacks, refrigerator magnets, a postcard with a beautiful image I can't bear to throw away . . . these are all good ideas.

Do you make soap? Perhaps you can approach locally run boutiques or salons or even coffee shops that have public restrooms and offer them free bars of your soaps to use in their facilities. Make up a small sign to hang in these bathrooms that will tell customers about your business and where they can buy your handmade soaps.

Make diaper bags? Contact a local daycare center that a family member or a friend recommends (or that perhaps you yourself use), and ask them to hold a raffle for a local children's charity with one of your bags as a prize. Everyone wins. The daycare has something to excite the parents, the charity gets some much-needed cash, and you expose your product to all the parents whose kids go to the daycare — people who may not ever have found your product otherwise.

Attracting Media Attention

So you're ready for more exposure. You're comfortable with your products and excited about the response you've had, so you want to get your business out there a bit more. What should you do? Why, contact the media of course! And nowadays that means not just the traditional print forms but online sources as well.

Online Media Opportunities

You've decided that you want to be featured on your favorite design or craft blog. Before you approach online editors, ask yourself a few important questions: What if they were to show-case you right away? Is your shop stocked? Are the items that you want them to feature on their site currently available? Is your website updated? Are you prepared for a possible rush of orders that may result from that kind of worldwide exposure? After all, the whole reason you want this kind of coverage is because you want to expose your business to more people, so you'll need to be ready to harness the power of both the Internet and media coverage. Are you?

If you can comfortably say yes to all those questions and are confident that you are indeed ready for the kind of exposure that the Internet can bring, what steps should you take to ensure that the editor will take notice of your work? For starters, make sure their blog is a good match for what you make. This is a good time to take note of the blogs and websites you frequent that have a lot in common with you since these are the best sites for you to approach. Obviously baby items won't generate any interest on a blog that focuses on fashion.

Okay, now that you're confident that you've chosen the best blogs to connect with, find their submission guidelines, and read them carefully. Some folks may want links to your website, some may want virtual press kits, and some just simply want an introductory e-mail with specifically sized photos included in the body (though some may not want you to send photos at all initially). These guidelines are in place for a reason, and the blog editor needs you to follow all the rules. You may be tempted to try to make yourself stand out by submitting more than what they ask for, but resist! Count on the quality and uniqueness of what you're selling to make you stand out.

DO YOUR HOMEWORK

Two of the most popular design blogs — decor8 (http://decor8blog.com) and Design*Sponge (www.designspongeonline.com) — each have one person at the helm, Holly Becker and Grace Bonney respectively. Neither Holly nor Grace has any staff to help them go through the hundreds of e-mails they receive requesting coverage, so respecting their submission guidelines will help you in your pursuit.

No matter what the guidelines are for the online editor of your choice, you'll need to send a well-crafted, thoughtful, and informative e-mail. Here are a few tips to make your e-mail shine. For starters, use the editor's first name when writing to them. If you're crafting a general e-mail that you plan on sending to lots of different editors, tweak each one personally. I was amazed at how many times blog editors told me that they get e-mails addressed to just the name of their website or to the impersonal heading "Dear Editor."

You are contacting real people with a passion for what they are doing, and they work hard to bring what they consider to be the best offerings from the design, art, and craft worlds to their audiences. These people work just as hard as you, and just like you they can get overwhelmed by their work. So following their guidelines and treating them like actual people are simple things that you can do to make sure you really connect.

This no doubt goes without saying, but present yourself well. Make sure you have spelled everything correctly. Use proper grammar. Do not treat your e-mail like a text message. Describe what you do fully, but keep it short and sweet. If you make earrings, small paintings, and table lamps using found objects, be sure to include information about all of these things. Perhaps the editor you're approaching doesn't cover jewelry, but she might be interested to know about all the things you do with recycled and repurposed items.

Make sure the links that you put in the body of the e-mail work. Perhaps try sending the e-mail first to a friend even or to yourself to ensure everything is working properly. You can also make your links look better by using some basic HTML. This would give you a working hot link in your e-mail that simply says "stationery" or "needle-felted animals" instead of a long, unsightly string of characters or symbols that creates a Web link.

Approaching Print Media

A great way to boost your sales is to get some press coverage. Whether it's a story about your business or whether something you make is featured in a product roundup on the glossy pages of your favorite magazine, getting press is one of the best ways for the world to learn more about you and want what you have to sell. Getting this kind of coverage just requires a little effort on your part — after which you should have no trouble finding your name in print.

Newspapers

Does your town have a newspaper or a local alternative weekly? If so, start paying attention to who writes the business or product stories, and either give them a call or send them a well-thought-out e-mail. Let them know who you are and what you're doing and what kind of community you serve, and offer them your story. If you send an e-mail, remember to include links to your shop or your blog, and attach some photos of your work to generate more interest.

Just as when you contact online editors, you need to be prepared. What is your hook? Why should the media want to cover you? Try to think of different angles that would make an article about you interesting. If you live in a small town, an account of a person who runs a craft business from home, even if it's a spare-time endeavor, may well be a story that your local paper would want to cover if you make your story appealing enough.

When you're reading articles online or in print about other crafters or artists, take note as to what the story is actually about. These are called "hooks" or "angles," and you'll need to offer one to a writer to get them interested in you.

Maybe your angle is you use sweaters you find at the thrift store to make blankets for babies, some of which you donate to your local pediatric center. Possibly you fell in love with rabbits after you rescued an injured one, and now your line of stationery is bunny-themed. Or perhaps after you had your first child, you decided to design the perfect diaper bag. All of these are hooks — the foundation on which a reporter can build a story.

Magazines

Think you don't have a hook? I'll bet you do. However, if you are indeed short on hooks, try just getting something you create featured in a gift guide or a magazine. Being featured in a magazine is a big deal and really exciting. Needless to say, an article or feature on your product can draw a lot of attention to your business. As you look through your favorite magazines, you may wonder how people wind up being featured. While there is no magic formula for getting print coverage, you can do certain things to see if there is any interest out there for what you make.

First of all, research what magazines your target audience reads. Once you have a good idea of what magazines your specific market likes, get copies and look through them to make sure they highlight products like yours. Think big here because you never know. If a magazine focuses on country-style decorating and seems to mostly feature layouts of interiors, even though you make dog leashes, the magazine might still be interested in showing them. They probably have a regular shopping or new-goods column, and that might just be the right place for one of the goodies you make for pampered pooches.

Getting featured in a national magazine can be a little more work than getting featured in your hometown newspaper, but it's well worth the effort. For starters, find out who the market editor is for your target publication. The market editor is in charge of a particular area of the market; market editors can focus on fashion, accessories, or pretty much any other kind of niche in an industry. Don't be afraid to approach these folks. They wouldn't have a magazine without stories to write — and the world is so big! They need you to provide them with content. They are looking for what's next or what's trendy, and when you bring a great product or story to them, you are lightening their load. Simply get in touch. Mail them a letter, including all of your information, or submit a press kit, which can sometimes include a sample of your work.

To find out where to send a letter, look on the magazine's masthead (the printed column somewhere at the beginning of the magazine that lists all of the staff), and figure out whom you want to contact. Call the magazine and ask for the correct snail mail or e-mail address for the person you want to be in touch with. (Often that information is available on the magazine's website.) It's just that easy. You may not hear back right away, but feel free to follow up within a month or six weeks from your first communication. Don't be a pest about it, but it's totally fine to send a friendly reminder.

Bear in mind that magazines have long the lead times: submit your amazing egg ornaments in the fall and holiday-themed wrapping paper in the summer.

FROM THE CREATIVE COLLECTIVE: NATALIE ZEE DRIEU

We get our story ideas through submissions from crafters and our pool of writers. There are two ways to get published on CRAFT: either we link to a project on a crafter's blog or site, or a crafter will write an exclusive project for us. We have a form on our site for submissions (Suggest a Site) as well as one for project pitches. Otherwise, an idea comes from an editor on our team and created by him or her for the site.

Send Samples

I encourage you to send samples of your work to editors or editorial assistants if you can. If you are going to send an unsolicited sample and you want it returned, include a self-addressed, sufficiently stamped envelope with a request to return your items, but you need to know that getting back samples that weren't requested isn't guaranteed.

If a printed publication is interested in using one of your products in a photo shoot, they will contact you and tell you exactly what they need. If you have the requested product available, great! If not, be up front about it. Tell them what you do have, and ask what their lead time is. If they have any wiggle room in their schedule, you may have the time to make exactly what they are looking for. If not, convince them to take something equally wonderful.

The publication should give you their shipping information and tell you what carrier to use. (In most cases when product is requested, you should not have to cover the cost of shipping, so make sure you ask them for this information.) Then you simply send out your craft along with an invoice or a fact sheet detailing what you're sending. Make sure you include all the information they may want to print, like the product details, the retail cost, and where the item can be purchased.

Putting Together a Press Kit

Exactly what are these mysterious "press kits" we've been talking about? And what is the difference between a physical press kit and a virtual one? First of all, having a press kit is not a necessity when you're a small business. As you grow your business, you may want to develop one, but if you don't have one now, don't sweat it. Though if you want to get going on one, a press kit is simply a way to give a complete overview of your company. Following are the basic elements of any complete press kit:

- ▸▸ **A fact sheet.** This gives the history of your company, including biographies of the most important people involved in your business — even if that most important person is just you. This is not like a personal résumé, but it can include where you went to school (if that is relevant to what you're doing now) and why you started your company. Your biography may also include a picture of you if you'd like. You may be thinking that your fact sheet and biography will wind up being close to the same thing, and that's okay, too. Just make sure all the required information you need is there.

➤➤ **Copies of any past press coverage.** If you've been interviewed or featured on any of the bigger blogs, you can include those articles.

➤➤ **A line sheet.** This is a sheet of everything you make, including the retail price. (If you were sending a line sheet out for a wholesale account, you would include your wholesale prices.)

➤➤ **A one sheet detailing what makes your wares unique.** This goes back to the hooks we talked about earlier. What makes your company stand out? Make sure you not only present a pretty package but a newsworthy one as well.

➤➤ **Photos of what you make.** If you can, include high-quality images of your product. You can also include a CD with hi-res images as well as the all-important business card.

➤➤ **Other marketing materials.** These would include brochures, promotional postcards, and the like.

You may be tempted to do something wacky to make your press kit stand out. Restrain yourself. Sending your press kit in a normal type of folder is best. Editors get a lot of these and, well, you know what a jumble of clutter a desk can become, right? Do these people a favor and send them something flat that they can easily stack or slip onto a shelf. Remember, though, that folders can be custom made, so use your crafty skills to figure out how to get the feeling of *you* into or onto your kit.

Remember your branding. The materials in your press kit should match the overall look and feel of your company. Make sure your logo and contact information are on every single thing you include in your kit. If one of your inserts were to get separated from the kit and someone picked it up, they should easily be able to tell who it belongs to.

Virtual Press Kits

A virtual press kit is pretty much the same thing as a printed one, except you deliver all the information electronically. If you are sending out a virtual kit, make sure that all of your links look good. Use simple HTML code to shorten your links so that someone can just click on a word and be taken to the online site where the information lives. You can even have a virtual press kit available as a PDF download on your website. Also, make sure that you have hi-res photos available for people to download.

Some people don't like to open attachments, so make sure what you send through e-mail is as user-friendly as possible.

Writing Press Releases

A press release is a targeted way to communicate major news about your company to the press at large. Note the word *major*. Only consider sending a press release if you have really big news to share with the whole world. (You might think you need a press release if you are introducing a new line at the beginning of a season, but a postcard with photos may do just as well.)

You may be able to drum up some press-worthy buzz if you time your news with a relevant local event. For instance, if you make reusable snack and lunch bags, then a well-timed release to your local news outlets around Earth Day may well be of interest to them.

There are many different schools of thought on formatting a press release, but the basics are:

➤ Your contact information should be printed along the top of the release, including the date.

➤ Give the release a title, which can be catchy but has to be to the point.

➤ Double-space your release so that it's easier to read.

➤ Try to keep your release to one page.

➤ Make sure to mention that you have photos available on request — and then make sure you really *do* have photos that relate to your news.

- Have someone you trust double-check your work (you don't want any mistakes, and it needs to be clear and to the point; having a second pair of eyes to help you edit can be really helpful).

- Include the five Ws: who, what, why, when, and where — and most, if not all, of this information should be in the first paragraph (a person should be able to glance quickly at the release and know everything they need to know about your news).

The landscape of public relations is changing quickly, and advice on using press releases to improve your sales and raise awareness of your business can be conflicting. In the olden days, all press releases were sent in the mail, addressed to the appropriate editor. Then came faxing, and now e-mail is in the mix. Some editors still prefer to receive a hard-copy release. If you have a specific media target in mind, call ahead to see if the editor you're interested in accepts press releases by e-mail.

Like any other professional communication you send out into the world, your press release should be addressed to a specific person — the release itself doesn't have to say Dear Ms. So and So, but if you're mailing a hard copy, the envelope should be personally addressed, and your fax cover sheet should be addressed this way, too. The same goes for e-mailed releases. Investigate your local media outlets (newspapers, TV stations, and regional magazines) to find editorial contacts.

So what happens after you send a press release out into the world? If you send it to a specific editor, hopefully they'll be intrigued by it. They will either call you to write a full story or request photos, or they can run the release as it is, after they make any editorial changes they deem necessary. Sometimes you may not hear back at all; even if your story is printed, no one is obligated to call you and tell you what day it will be running. How is that possible? Often press releases are used for filler copy in newspapers and regional magazines, and they can be printed exactly the way you send them (minus your contact information, of course). That's why you really need to think about what you're trying to communicate — and whether your news is actually newsworthy.

After giving the corporate world a try for a decade, Holly Becker decided to chuck the 9-to-5 grind for a more creative life (not to mention more flexible hours), with the hope of combining her love of interior design with writing for magazines. A desire to help a handbag-designer friend to get her goods seen online led Holly to start a blog. Now, three years later, decor8 is successful beyond her wildest dreams, and her blog topics go way beyond finding the best couch for a space. Her readers are treated to heartfelt, intimate con-nections, examining such concepts as creativity, inspiration, and empowerment, among others.

How do people best attract your attention when e-mailing you in hopes of getting coverage on decor8?

Brevity and great photos are key. I appreciate personal emails that address me by name. I'd rather have key information listed using bullet points over elaborate press releases or introductions. The perfect pitch includes a quick introductory para-graph, their full name, product and company name, links to where they can be found online (i.e., website, blog, shop), and a few photos show-ing their work — those shot in natural daylight that are no larger than 800 pixels work best. A picture is worth a thousand words, so spend time on taking solid product photos.

(Q&A continued on next page)

125

What information do you find helpful in a press kit? Do you accept paper press kits?

Yes, I accept them, but paper press kits are not helpful personally, because I do not require high res photos for decor8 since I am not a print publication. I encourage small business owners who approach blog-gers to focus more on presenting strong product photos over elaborate presentations. Remember, your port-folio is only as strong as your weakest photo, so make sure all of your prod-uct shots are your personal best. It's better to send a few great ones than lots of mediocre ones. I encourage those who want to pitch to me to first look at my blog content; if they can imagine fitting in with my overall theme and aesthetic, they should by all means e-mail their submission.

What makes you responsive to someone?

First, e-mails that address me by my name! There is nothing sweeter in a sea of submissions addressed to Heather, Becky, and my favor-ite, "Decor8 Team" than to see an e-mail that simply begins with "Dear Holly." Next, I appreciate if they take the time to tell me that they have decided to contact me first to share a product because they think it would be of interest to me and my readers. Those who consider my blog content and overall aesthetic before reaching out always impress me, and so they rise to the top of the submissions pile. (I read around 3,000 weekly.) I'm very visual, so in addition to being considerate and friendly, great photographs catch my eye instantly. If I connect to what is being pre-sented, I then read the e-mail, visit the links, and consider the bio, which is usually found on their website or blog. If the e-mail is short and sweet and contains all of the vitals, I may write about them within a day or two.

How do you decide what to feature on your website?

This is the easiest part of what I do because I either connect to some-thing or I don't. My blog is a very personal reflection of what's inside of me — if a product doesn't fit my sen-sibility I look for those that do. I'm always searching for those who may have little to no knowledge of how powerful blogging can be to their business. To convince and encourage them to start pitching to blogs, I'll write about them on decor8. It's my baptism-by-fire approach, I guess. But this little push suddenly introduces them to thousands of people worldwide, and this level of exposure is often just the boost they need.

What piece of advice would you offer a crafter/artist looking to gain national attention for their work?

Edit, edit, edit! Hone your skills to develop a strong cohesive portfolio. It is better to show a smaller strong body of work than a chaotic mix of many things. Join a local crafting club or design group to make a few friends who may be able to give you an honest critique, but most of all support and a fresh perspective. Find a mentor who is not in the same business, to avoid feelings of competition or jealousy. Show your work locally. It's easy to test the market at a local arts-and-crafts event by setting up a booth and connecting with the public. Gauge what the overall response is and listen more to the constructive criticism than to the glowing reviews.

Once you feel proud of your product line, contact bloggers and magazine editors, and if they are not interested, always ask why. Their insights may be exactly what you need to hear!

Your readers are treated to more than just design ideas, products, and eye candy for the home. You choose to take your connection deeper, with series on creativity and the like. Why do this?

My goal is for those who read decor8 to walk away feeling positive, inspired, and more creative — and to think about something in a fresh, new way. I want them to feel motivated to try new things, but also I believe that there is more to life than material objects and the perfect floor plan to enjoy being at home. Decorating alone is not the only way to give a room warmth and comfort, but that those living there need to be happy and feel a sense of joy and accomplishment, hope, and are reaching personal goals and experience good relations within their family. This is my wish for everyone and why I choose to take my connections with readers deeper.

Chapter 8

MORE ONLINE MARKETING NETWORKS

Your audience can be reached in so many ways these days, and the evolution of available means is ongoing. If I had written this book even two years ago, resources like Twitter and Facebook wouldn't even be on our radar. Newer technology like podcasts and video blogs are just some of the ways that we can further reach out and connect with people across the world. Taking a chance and testing out these kinds of communications can be fun and informative.

Podcasting

One of my favorite ways to spend time is by listening to a great podcast with a focus on crafting. I simply download the latest podcasts that I subscribe to into my MP3 player via iTunes, grab my headphones, and settle in for a lot of crafty goodness.

Huh? What?

If you didn't understand any or all of that, don't worry. Whether podcasting is totally unfamiliar to you or whether you already have a few favorites you listen to regularly, no matter where you are in your podcast education, this section will surely clear things up for you.

An always-evolving new medium, podcasting is an awesome way to connect with your market. Think of a podcast as a radio show that focuses solely on topics that you are interested in. As with all techniques, there is always something new to learn, and if you delve into this amazing way to communicate, I promise you'll have a good time.

Why should you bother learning something new? Especially if you already have a website? Well, think of podcasting as a way to complement your existing marketing efforts. It is simply a new way for you to reach out to your target audience and your community.

Podcast Basics

To begin podcasting, some basic equipment is needed: a computer and a microphone. Yep, that's it. If you have a recent computer, it may have a built-in mike; if not, you can get a USB mike for around $30 that will connect to your computer. Add to that some software that lets your computer record sound and even edit audio (one option: Audacity, a free, easy-to-learn program offered at www.audacity. sourceforge.net), and you're good to go. (Note: Avoid online services that promote using your phone to record a podcast; the sound quality stinks!) If after you've been podcasting a while you find that you're loving the idea, you can choose to upgrade your mike and also purchase a preamplifier, which will improve the sound quality of your broadcasts.

Podcast Tips from Diane Gilleland

- Creating your own podcasts is not the only way to benefit from them; listening to podcasts is a great way to learn new things, get inspired, and even relax.
- It takes time for a podcast (or blog) to grow an audience and become a marketing engine for your business. I'd recommend that new podcasters give themselves at least six months before they decide to give up.

With your equipment in place, you'll next need a site on the Web where folks can listen to your words of wisdom. Free hosting services (PodBean — www.podbean.com — is one) are an option, but, just like TV broadcasting on the networks, your podcast won't be commercial-free. In exchange for the freebie hosting, the service will likely tack on a message about their service to the start of your podcast. Alternately, you can enjoy podcasts without commercials from a hosting service like Libsyn (www.libsyn.com). The most popular hosting service, Libsyn (which is short for Liberated Syndication) offers monthly plans that range from $5 to $60, depending on the server storage space you require.

It isn't necessary to have an MP3 player to listen to podcasts. Using a service like iTunes enables listeners to tune in through a computer whenever they like.

What Should Your Podcast Be About?

Before jumping in with your USB microphone in hand, try listening to those podcasts that most appeal to you. These days there is a lot of variety in podcasts. Some let you listen in on a conversation between friends as they talk about their mutual craft pursuits. Some are interview-based, with the host talking to experts in the craft field they are most interested in. Other podcasts are like stories, where the host sort of blogs out loud if you will. Find a style that appeals to you and that you think will work for your community, and then dig in!

Once you take the plunge and record a podcast, you'll need to put it out there. You can create a podcast button and post it to your blog or Twitter about your podcast or mention it in your newsletter. You can also register your podcast with various directories and hope that people will find it that way. Just put the word out as you would for any other endeavor, and over time you'll build an audience.

Social Media

Social media is growing in popularity and changing the way we relate to one another and the way we do business. Taking part in these online social groups will enrich what you do, and if you're anything like me, you'll enjoy it.

The online landscape has changed so much in just the past year or two, who knows what options will be available a few years from now, so I'm just going to cover the basics here. As I write this, Facebook, Twitter, Flickr, and YouTube are the big ones.

FROM THE CREATIVE COLLECTIVE: TARA SWIGER

Being part of the crafting community has inspired me to learn about social media, to blog, to Twitter. And all that communication with the community has led to writing for magazines, traveling across the country for craft shows, and some great friendships with other fiberistas.

Twitter

Twitter is a micro-blogging website, which is to say that the length of the message is extremely restricted. Users, or Twitterers, can sign up for a free account, then reach out to people around the world — as long as they keep their "tweet" at or under 140 characters, including spaces and punctuation. So Twitter is a place for you to share your thoughts in a few words. Sounds tough, but it is actually supereasy, and using it is an incredibly effective way to market your business. Believe it or not, there is a lot you can convey and learn from a 140-characters limit. Twitter is all about having a conversation, and it's a great way to build a community around yourself and your work.

Twitter is fun and easy to use, but the trick is to remember the old adage about getting too much of a good thing. The overall Twitter community is pretty clear about a few things they like and a few things they don't like. You'll find loads more information online about how to utilize Twitter and how to be an upstanding member of the community. Perhaps

FROM THE CREATIVE COLLECTIVE: LIZ SMITH

The best thing Twitter has done for me is connect me to other crafters online. They feature me on their blogs, pass around my links, and let me know which shows I should check out. I have also gotten to know other crafters I might have overlooked in person (maybe they don't make something that interests me) but really like once I see their personality on social media, and I hope that works conversely for me.

Twitter Tips

As with any other online communication, like e-mail, people don't like to be spammed. So don't use all of your Twitter time to promote yourself and your business. Twitter is a two-way street, and you need to be supportive to get support.

This is all up to you, of course, but most people don't like auto followers. That means just because you follow someone, they may not immediately follow you back. They may take the time to check in on you and read your past tweets before becoming one of your followers.

In the same vein, lots and lots of followers dislike automatic direct messages. That is a service that sends a direct message (DM) to anyone who follows you. So if I start to follow you and right away I see a DM from you, it can't really be a personal message because you clearly don't know me yet.

If you decide to follow someone, it is considered a polite courtesy to tweet them and introduce yourself.

Tweeting is not like texting. People will really appreciate it if you use proper punctuation and spell your words completely if you can.

If the information you want to convey is longer than 140 characters, maybe Twitter isn't the right place to post it. Consider writing a blog and linking back to it on Twitter if you need more room.

Picking an Avatar
for Social Media Websites

An avatar is the little picture that accompanies most online profiles these days. What to choose? It depends on your school of thought. Some people like an avatar to be a photo of you. They like seeing the human being behind the company. Some people feel more comfortable carrying on a conversation, even one that takes place online, if they can picture whom they're talking to.

You might prefer to have a product associated with your business name. A good example of using a product as an avatar is that used by Tara Swiger, a member of my Creative Collective. If you look for her on Twitter, her name is @blondechicken, and her avatar is one of her beautiful skeins of hand-spun yarn. Blonde Chicken is the name of her Etsy store, and her website is called Blonde Chicken Boutique, so she has a whole branding thing going on. Or consider using your logo if you have one. Whatever you ultimately choose as your avatar, it's best to use the same one for all your avatar needs. If you use a Gmail e-mail account or have other active accounts that will display the picture of your choice, use one that represents your business.

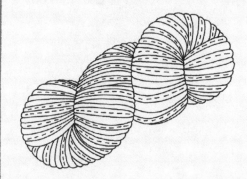

the best thing about Twitter is it most likely won't be as cluttered with your actual friends and family, and if you have willpower, you can use it quickly and easily, and it's free. Plus it's the simplest application to use.

SIGNING UP FOR TWITTER

When you sign up for your free account at www.twitter.com, you'll need to choose a user name. Be careful when selecting your name; you don't want it to be too many characters since they count in those 140 characters when someone is tweeting or responding to you. You can use your business name if you like because Twitter gives you the option to add a professional name as well. For example, @handmademarketplace could be my twitter name, but I also could be searchable by Kari Chapin if I wanted to be. The title of my book is too long to be my Twitter name because it eats up 19 characters plus the @ sign. The @ sign needs to be included — that is how people find you. When someone tweets you directly, they will have to type in "@you" — and remember: symbols, numbers, punctuation, and spaces count as characters. In the example above, "Kari Chapin" only shows up when you search for me in this case. You can search for people either by their name or business name.

FROM THE CREATIVE COLLECTIVE: LEAH KRAMER

It's always a great rule of thumb to give as much as you get out of an online community. So don't just ask questions; be sure to answer other people's questions when you can. This can be hard if you're very busy, but it's worth it because it's what makes online communities successful.

HOW CAN TWITTER HELP YOUR BUSINESS?

Simple. It allows you to reach a ton of people from all around the world without relying on them finding your normal blog or website or your online shop. What are some business-enhancing things you could tweet about? Let's see . . . If you've gotten some excellent press lately, post a link to it; people can click through to learn more. Or when you update your shop, let people know. Stuck on a problem? Ask your followers for help. Have a question about supplies or techniques? Post a tweet, and watch the advice roll in. The possibilities are many, and Twitter is a free and easy way to not only market yourself but expand your community, make new friends, and gain insights about your interests in a whole new way.

Facebook

You probably already have a personal Facebook account for yourself, but how about one for your business? Facebook can spread your name to similar crafters, and you can also keep people informed with posts, pics, and giveaways. But its most beneficial use would be the contacts generated. Just as you personally stay in touch with old classmates, friends, and family, Facebook is another great tool to let you see and be seen by your target audience and other crafters.

FROM THE CREATIVE COLLECTIVE: MEGAN RISLEY

I post shop updates to my personal Facebook page, and it has made a difference in my sales. People who otherwise wouldn't know about my online shop are quicker to buy from me because they know me through Facebook.

Facebook offers businesses a chance to get in on the action with a feature called a Fan Page. Fan Pages are free and easy to build. Also, Fan Pages are viewable by the general public whereas your personal Facebook page is not. That means anyone can become a "fan" of your crafts — and that's a good thing! You can post photos of your work and link to all the places where you are selling your crafts. You can also send updates and relevant news to people who subscribe to your page. Easy! Also, a Fan Page can be viral in some cases. Whenever you post an update to your page, it will show up in the stream of everyone who has become a fan of yours. And if they haven't turned notifications off, then anyone who looks at their stream can see your update, thereby exposing your crafts to new people.

One way to make your Fan Page more interactive is to encourage people who have bought things from you to tag themselves with your product. Maybe even make a contest out of it, with each month's best-tagged picture getting a small bag of goodies. This will not only add more pictures to your profile where your items are tagged, but it'll also show real people in real situations really enjoying your wares. That definitely helps to win over someone who may have just stumbled on your page for the first time, or might just sway someone who is already familiar with your goods but has been on the fence about buying. Photos of happy customers smiling while holding up your crafts go a long way.

Remember: The more active you are with your Facebook page (and any other marketing, for that matter), the more interest you'll generate in your products.

YouTube

Another social media site that can be relevant to your crafting and community building is YouTube. You can create commercials showing off your product or a new line. Do you have a simple small item you don't mind demonstrating how to make? Create a how-to video. The most important thing is to make sure all of your videos are tagged with your name, your business, and your product name. That way someone who tries to Google you or your business will be sure to find your videos as well. Linking your YouTube clips with your website and Facebook helps to create a chain of information for potential customers to easily find, follow, and become fans of your work.

Small video cameras are more affordable than ever these days. Perhaps you know someone who has one you can borrow, just to try it out. Making a video or a "vlog" (visual blog or video blog) is pretty easy to do. No one expects you to produce Hollywood-style quality, and you can make a video that is short and sweet. Feeling camera-shy? You don't even

have to appear in the video. Instead, show off your studio space, or film your booth before a craft show, or take a visual tour of your favorite crafty haunts.

The possibilities of communicating through video are endless and enormously fun! If you decide to make a video, it's both free and easy to upload it to YouTube. Once you've posted your video, be sure to tag it appropriately, and then post links to it on the other social-media sites where you're active.

Flickr

Flickr is a photo-sharing community, and anyone can join for free — but what you can upload is restricted with a free account. A year's membership is around $25 as of this writing and well worth it, plus you can write it off!

Flickr, in case you don't know yet, is incredible. Many of the people interviewed for this book say that Flickr is one of their main sources of inspiration. Spend even just a short amount of time on the site, and you'll soon see why. Flickr is also a great way to expose loads of people to your work. There are more than 500,000 groups on Flickr, and a whole lot of them revolve around crafts. A quick search showed that the most popular online marketplaces are all represented, and I couldn't find a single craft that didn't pull up a group. This means whether you work with appliqué, or if quilling is more your style, you can find a group out there who shares your passion.

SIGNING UP ON FLICKR

Simply sign up, and start uploading!

Wait! It can't be that easy, can it? Truthfully there is more to it, but it's all really easy. First decide what you want your user name to be. For branding purposes, I'm going to suggest you go with your business name or a name that identifies your business. Remember, it is best to have all of these names and their corresponding avatars match. Speaking of avatars, you'll need one for your Flickr account, too.

Flickr allows you to have a member profile. Again, this is one of those places where your information needs to be consistent for branding purposes. Be sure to link to your online shop, your website, and even your Facebook Fan Page.

ORGANIZING AND TAGGING YOUR PHOTOS

Flickr allows you to do three different things with your uploaded photos. You can title and tag them, create sets and

FROM THE CREATIVE COLLECTIVE: KIM WERKER

When it comes to using social media, my best advice would be to be honest. All the time. Authenticity is the single most important currency in online life. Share about your process, your products, your relevant work experiences. Follow the golden rule, and treat other people as you want to be treated.

add them to sets, and/or add them to groups. Ideally you want to do all three.

Titling and Tagging: The titles of your photos need to clearly state the designated name of your item. So if the sweater you're selling is called "Purple Delight Turtleneck" in your online store, your photo should share the same name.

Next up is tagging your photo. Tags are simply descriptive search terms. They are your chance to describe the photo in detail, which helps when people are searching based on words that interest them. Online sites usually limit the number of tags you can add to a photo, to help make searching more targeted. Astonishingly, Flickr allows at least 75 tags per photo, but I'm sure you would be hard-pressed to come up with that many descriptors — and you probably don't want to. Think about the things that make your item special as a place to start with your tags. If other things stand out in your photo, move on to those next. For example, the photo of your purple sweater may have been taken on a vintage dress form in your dining room with your paint-by-numbers collection hanging on the wall behind it, and the yarn you used in the sweater was organic hand-spun cotton. So your tags may look like this:

- Purple (its color)
- Sweater (what it is)
- Knitted (what you did)
- Clothing (what a sweater is)
- Organic yarn (type of yarn)
- Hand spun (something special about the yarn)
- Size XL (size of the sweater)
- Chixon on Etsy (name of your shop and where sweater is for sale)
- Handmade (because it is)
- Etsy (where it is for sale comes up by itself)
- Paint-by-numbers (something of interest)
- Vintage dress form (something of interest)

Although the paint-by-numbers paintings and dress form have nothing to do with selling your item, they are things that people may search for — and could be a way to lead people who didn't even know they wanted a purple sweater straight to your website.

Creating Sets: You can also group photos into sets, which is a very helpful feature. For example, you can have a set of all the sweaters you've knitted, and when someone looks in the set, they can see a complete body of work. It is also helpful when it comes to linking your work because you'll have one link that can lead someone to a number of your sweater photos at once.

If you create a slideshow on your blog or website, you can have the focus be of a set of your choice, which is nice if you're showing new work or trying to push something in particular.

Adding to Groups: Now that your photos have been titled and tagged, you can add your tagged photo to some groups. To add photos to groups, you need to belong to those groups. Spend some time using Flickr's search feature to find some groups that are good matches for you. Groups for just about every single thing you can imagine exist on Flickr. If you're into crafting with seashells, there is a group for you. Ditto if you sell your items on Etsy or Artfire or create fan work inspired by the Boston Red Sox.

I know we've just covered a lot of information, and it may seem daunting if you're unfamiliar with these online tools. If you're concerned that you're already strapped for time or feel like you spend too much time on the computer as it is, relax! The beauty of all of these options is that you can pick and choose what suits you and your goals the best. If you don't want to create a podcast or vlog, you can just listen or watch them instead!

All of these options offer lasting value to the community, and no matter how you participate, you'll experience benefits.

Known to the crafting community as "Sister Diane," Diane Gilleland describes herself as a "big crafty geek." Via her wonderful podcast, CraftyPod, and her blog, she shares information about projects and ideas from her fellow crafters and also holds interviews with interesting artisans. Diane has been featured in CRAFT and Sew News magazines, and on the web site CraftStylish, and authors her own craft e-books. Here she shares some of her thoughts about podcasting.

What led you to podcasting?

I have spent thousands of hours crafting while listening to National Public Radio. I love making things while listening. My partner, who is very tech-savvy, discovered podcasts about four years ago and sent me some links. I loved the idea of making my own radio shows and soon began producing a little show called *SpinsterSpin*, in conjunction with a website I had at the time. (For the record, it was a show for women who choose not to marry or have children.) After a couple months, I was hooked on audio editing — something I had never tried before but found mesmerizing. And one day it occurred to me: There should be a podcast about crafts! So *CraftyPod* was born, a show about crafting that people could listen to while crafting! The idea captivated me.

How did you decide there was value in it?

I love the fact that anybody can make their own media now. We are no longer limited to the stories, images, and sounds that mainstream editors deem important. We can all tell our own little story, put it out to the world, and find the handful of like-minded souls who can really understand what we're saying. That's incredibly powerful.

How has podcasting enhanced your own craft business?

The podcast has led me to so many opportunities! First, the very act of interviewing people has allowed me to develop relationships with a wide variety of creative folks, and those conversations have continued well beyond the podcast. And when listeners comment on the shows, that leads to even more connections. As a result of the podcast (and my blog), I was invited to write an article for *CRAFT* magazine. This then led me to write for other publications and websites. One of the interviews I conducted led to the interviewee hiring me to produce some freelance podcasts for his company.

How do you decide what topics to cover in your podcast?

I podcast about what fascinates me. My podcast is a 100 percent volunteer effort, and I have no interest in taking any sponsorship money for it. The minute I take on sponsors, I become beholden to them, and they have a say in what shows up on the podcast. I'd rather make it an authentic statement of what interests me about this amazing craft community. I think this leads to a far more interesting show, which in turn leads to more new opportunities.

In general, I like to cover stories that have some larger, lasting value for crafters. In other words, I rarely interview people solely to say, "Wow, you're so great; how did you get started?" Instead, I want to ask them about their life lessons or areas of real expertise. I tend to be interested in metastories about the culture of crafters.

What advice would you give to people just beginning to dip their toes into the world of podcasting?

Listen to lots of different podcasts, and make note of what you like and what you don't like about each one. This will help you decide your format — is it long or short? Will you interview people, or will the show be just you? Will you have a serious tone or a funny one? Starting out with a

143

definite format in mind really helps you focus as you climb the learning curve. I'd also recommend giving some thought to what subjects you will (and will not) cover in your show. I actually write out a script for every podcast. I've had to practice long and hard so I can read those scripts out loud without sounding like I'm reading, but having my material prepared helps me keep the show very focused and information-rich.

How can podcasting help crafters with their business?

It's a particularly lovely tool for artists and crafters for two reasons. First, it allows you to connect with your online audience in a way that's slightly more personal and intimate than a blog. If I read your blog, I can enjoy your words, but I can feel even more like I know you if I can hear your voice. Second, lots of creative people listen to podcasts while they do other things. So if they listen to your podcast while they commute, you're providing them with some welcome relief from that grind. If they're listening while they make their art, you're a creative companion. It's a lovely gift to people.

How did you spread the word to get listeners?

Well, back when I first started, I submitted my podcast feed to iTunes, Podcast Alley, and a lot of other podcast directories. Nowadays I'd recommend submitting only to iTunes, which is very easy to do. (Go to the iTunes Store's Podcast section, and look for the Submit a Podcast link.) In addition, I'd recommend having a blog for your podcast. This gives your show an identifiable home on the Web and also gives you a place to post "show notes" with each episode of your podcast (links to any people, places, or things you've mentioned plus a few lines on what the show is about). If you have a blog, you can also then go out and comment on other people's blogs and leave the URL for your blog with your comment. That helps draw others to your blog and podcast.

It takes time to build an audience — it took about a year for CraftyPod to gain momentum. But don't worry; just keep making podcasts. Once you've built up a fan base, they'll go back and listen to your older shows.

PART

3

GETTING DOWN TO SELLING

Chapter 9

THE CRAFT FAIR SCENE

C raft fairs — whether major regional events, local art bazaars, or even tables in your neighborhood church basement — are great places to set up shop and sell your stuff. Not only can you build community around your brand, but you can also make new friends, meet new customers, get valuable feedback about your line, and earn some money while you're at it. Not to mention grow your mailing list, promote yourself, study up on the competition, and get new ideas.

First Things to Know

What do you need to know before jumping into the craft-fair scene? How do you find out where craft fairs are being held? How do you know if they're any good? How will you set up your booth? How much inventory should you have? What if you don't get accepted? What if you *do* get accepted? Oh, my. There's so much to think about!

Let's take a step back and start at the beginning. The path from your studio or workspace to a sales booth or table at a crafts venue can be a long but rewarding one. First of all, do you want to sell in a public venue? This may seem like a no-brainer, but it's actually something you need to consider. You already know that creating your products is hard work. You already know that maintaining your online store (assuming you have one already) is a lot of work. You already know that keeping track of your bookkeeping, feedback, and supplies is hard work. Craft fairs represent a whole other kind of hard work. Strenuous physical labor, lonely hours, long stretches of time with no bathroom breaks, hours standing outside in lousy weather, people not interested in buying what you have to sell, and, well, did I mention the hard work?

But no doubt you're a go-getter who is up for anything that'll help your business, in which case the above paragraph hasn't scared you off, right? Good! With the fair warnings (no pun intended) out of the way, let's get started.

Finding Fairs

Decide which craft fairs interest you. Cast your research net far and wide — the sky's the limit here. It's okay to think big when it comes to craft fairs, and you should use all of your resources. Do you live in Denver, but your best friend lives in Brooklyn? Are you from Raleigh, but your parents moved to Des Moines? Research craft fairs in all areas where you have personal connections. Every fair that happens near you or someone you know is a cost-effective option if you can stay with friends and relatives and avoid paying for a hotel. Which isn't to say that you shouldn't research a fair located nowhere near anyone you know, but obviously free accommodations beats having to pay for a bed — not to mention, hey, free labor if your friends or family agree to help you out during the event.

There are many different ways to search for fairs. You can do a good old-fashioned (well, nowadays) Google search. You can scour the blogs and websites of crafters you admire, and see what fairs they attend. You can check out the ads in magazines that appeal to you, where some fairs are announced. You can call your county's chamber of commerce to see if any upcoming events are planned.

Or you can peruse the bulletin boards in art-supply stores and coffee shops for flyers announcing any happenings. Pretty much any place where people can post information, you should be able to find something.

Make a list called "Craft Fair Possibilities." This is just the start of your research. Now you need to gather as many facts as you can about the events you're considering. The more information you have, the easier it will be to decide which of these fair options are the right fit for you and your wares.

Good places to check out the fairs you're considering are forums of the online crafty places you hang out in. Search for people who have attended the fairs you're interested in, and read their feedback. Note both the positive and the negative feedback about a show. This feedback research should help you decide if you want to apply for specific fairs. Bear in mind that feedback is subjective. Reading about a few bad experiences someone else has had shouldn't be the one deciding factor as to whether or not a particular fair is right for you. Everybody has bad days and bad shows, so be mindful to take the negatives with a grain of salt. On the other hand, if many different people are repeating the same kind of negative things, this is something to take into consideration.

Evaluating Each Fair

When you've narrowed down your list to fairs that seem right for you, then what? Here's a list of things to consider:

>> At what time of year does the fair take place? Is it right before a holiday when people traditionally give or exchange presents?

This factor could affect the kind of business you do. If you knit winter hats or make letterpress Christmas, Hanukkah, or Kwanzaa cards, a show in the middle of the summer might not be the right one for you. However, if you make and design silk flower jewelry, a show just before Mother's Day might be a good thing.

>> What other kind of artisans are usually at this fair?

If you make earrings, and you can see from past vendor lists that loads of other earring makers sell at this event, it may not be the right fair for you. Or if you make arm warmers and this fair has a lot of high-end handcrafted furniture, your audience may not shop here. It is important to know your customer and to know if said customer will likely be at the event.

>> What is the event's background? Has it gotten bigger over the years? Smaller? What are the entry fees?

If an event is growing and the people in charge have to find bigger and better venues, it means the customers they're attracting are creating a demand, which is good news for you. Conversely, if an event is getting smaller, it may be because sufficient audience isn't attending. If the event has been going on for several seasons, it probably has a dedicated group of attendees, whereas if the event is brand new, however, have the organizers made projections about how many people will attend? Finally, consider the entry fees — some events are expensive, but if they put you in touch with lots of potential customers, they may be worth it.

Finding the answers may be as simple as digging deep on their website, so look there first; but if the answers you're looking for aren't evident after a thorough search of the website, contact the folks in charge, and politely ask them your questions. (Keep in mind that the creative folks planning the event are probably very busy. Planning and hosting a craft fair involves a lot of work, and they may not be able to get back to you right away.) You should ask the fair promoters the following questions:

- How are you spreading the word about the event?

- Where are you advertising?

- How many people can your venue hold?

- What kind of support are you able to offer vendors?

- Is there designated parking for vendors?

- How will the parking be for the customers?

Study the vendor guidelines. You will need to know about the allotted space size and what the timelines are. Fairs seem to have two different standards (which is not to say those are the only two options). Most places will either assign you a booth, usually 10 by 10 feet, or a table, which can be anywhere from 4 to 6 feet long. If you have a booth, a table and at least two chairs are generally provided for you. Sometimes you have an option to bring your own tables and chairs, or there can be an extra charge for the event staff to provide them for you. You can decide what's best for you when the time comes; just make sure you know what's what in advance.

A few more things about your booth space to consider are: Do you need electricity for your display? If so, can it be provided? Do you need wall space? If not, can you build and transport a freestanding unit? If the event is outdoors, is a tent included in your fee? If a tent isn't included, are you willing to buy or rent one? If you do decide to rent one, will the tent company drop it off and pick it up free of charge? And will assembly be included in the rental fee?

Loading in and packing out of craft fairs is probably the number one cause for vendors' frustration. Find out how much time you have to do both. Usually an event will open for vendors a few hours before the doors open to the public. This gives you time to unload your wares and set up. Make sure you know how the loading in/loading out process works, too. I've heard of some places asking vendors to wait up to two hours after the doors close to load up. You need to know because it affects the time you must spend at the event. Also, if you are paying yourself by the hour, these hours before and after a fair should be factored into your paycheck.

By now in your research you will know everything necessary to decide which fairs you want to apply to, having based your decision on all the important logistical factors. Hopefully you are excited and can't wait to apply to them — which is great because that's what comes next: It's time to put yourself out there and get your craft fair on.

The Fair Application Process

Each event you want to apply to will have "Vendor Guidelines" or something similarly titled. These can vary from fair to fair, so be sure to read each event's guidelines carefully, and follow the directions exactly.

The fine folks who organize the shows you want to be a part of are hardworking, creative individuals who are often volunteers. They came up with an idea and did all the legwork; they found an affordable venue, researched and paid for permits and

FROM THE CREATIVE COLLECTIVE: NATALIE ZEE DRIEU

To make a craft fair successful, there needs to be a good variety of products. Sometimes there's an overabundance of applications in one category. For the most part, I see this in the jewelry category. Sometimes there are too many vendors with the same kinds of style and products and just not enough spaces to accommodate everyone.

other necessary licenses, arranged for cleanup afterward, made posters and wrote press releases to advertise the event, and handled myriad other responsibilities I'm not even listing here. These people have to work around a ton of restrictions and the schedules of other people. They only need one thing from you: to respect the application they've created. Do what they ask and how they've asked you to do it. For example, if they want you to submit five photos, don't submit 10; and while we're on the photo tip, if they want you to send JPEGs of a certain size, do it — don't send PDF files just because that's what you already have on hand. And do not send organizers to your Flickr account or to your website to view photos of your wares unless they ask to receive your pics that way.

Also, don't take their time or their memories for granted. If you've applied to Awesome Craft Fair three years in a row, and you've been accepted three years in a row, don't assume the fourth year that they will remember you or know who you are. Put your best foot forward each and every time you apply to an event.

Usually vendor applications are simple and straightforward. You will most likely be asked for your contact information, an artist's statement or a short bio of yourself and your work, and images of your work. In other chapters we have discussed the importance of taking great photos and how to identify your brand. We'll touch on both of those things again here, although with a little more brevity.

Double-check the requirements for the artist's statement. A character statement may be needed, or the organizers may ask you for only a certain number of sentences. Your statement should fit the requirements exactly while expressing who you are and what your work is about. Remember that these people need to know about you and about what you do. If you can mention your creative process at all in your statement, you should. This is a craft show, after all, and *how* you make your items can be as important as *what* you make. If what you do in your daily life plays a big part with what you make, mention that, too. Same goes for your education if you feel it adds value to your work.

Incidentally, if you're a fan of the show and have attended before either as a shopper or as a vendor, mention that in your application. Remember how hard these fair organizers are working, so give them some props whenever possible.

Application Photos

More and more craft fairs are accepting links to photos online. Hopefully you have an online portfolio, but if you don't, it's easy to put one together (see box). No matter how show organizers accept your photos, though, they are all looking for the same thing: excellent pictures that accurately represent what you want to sell at their fair. Your photos should be as high quality as you can manage and give the organizers a good idea of what you and your crafts are all about.

Present a variety of what you do if you plan on selling different types of items. Say you make T-shirts, fabric wrist cuffs, and pillows. You should have one clear photo of each category. You don't have to get all fancy, with a professional light booth or Photoshop — just set up a space with lighting that works well for you, and get in there and take some good shots. Think about how you're styling your photos as well. Try taking some shots of the wrist cuff on an actual hand that is holding a bunch of

•••• Creating an Online Portfolio ••••

It's a cinch to create an online portfolio. Just group together photos of your very best work and have it ready to go at a moment's notice. If you have a Flickr account, you can simply create a set, and send that link directly to whomever needs it. Just make sure the group of photos is clean; don't let a picture of you with a lampshade on your head sneak in — unless, of course, you made the lampshade!

wildflowers. Show that pillow on your sofa. And have your stylish BFF model one of your T-shirts. Be mindful of the wonderful details you include in your work; if you hand-embroider your pillows and use a variety of stitches and thread sizes, make sure all those fine points are clearly evident. These photos can make or break your acceptance into an event. Consider this: There may be as many as three times as many applicants as there are available tables or booths — and each applicant may submit multiple photos of their wares. Therefore it's essential that your photos stand out and are memorable. What can you do?

Research, my friends. Poke around other crafters' photos and see what stands out to you, and then try to find a way to take your inspiration and put your own mark on it. Maybe a jewelry designer who works with raw natural materials displayed her necklaces on beautiful rocks. You could take that inspiration and find something else from nature to display your goods on, like a piece of driftwood or interesting tree branches. Or maybe you can show the size of your earrings by showcasing them beside a fresh flower. Better still, show what you make on an actual model. Get creative, but make sure that no matter what you make, your craft is the star of the shot, and your wares aren't overwhelmed by your display of choice.

Your Application Is Complete If . . .

Before you hit "send" on your application, ask yourself the following questions, and if you can answer yes to all, you're ready to go:

➤➤ If I were new to this craft, would I have a clear understanding of what it is from these photos?

➤➤ If I were new to this craft and saw it online, would these photos provide a good enough view of the product to inspire me to actually buy it?

➤➤ Is my product the main point of these photos?

Getting the Word

One of three options will await your application. You will be accepted (yes!), rejected (boo!), or put on a waiting list (huh?).

If you're accepted, get ready to both celebrate and do a bunch more hard work. If you were rejected, take a deep breath, pat yourself on the back for trying, and get ready to do a bunch more hard work. If you've been wait-listed, you should feel good about having passed the application process, but you also need to figure out exactly what that means to the people in charge, since being wait-listed can mean different things to different event organizers. Perhaps the people in charge are waiting to see if everyone who was accepted can actually attend. (Maybe they are waiting to see if everyone can pay the fees.)

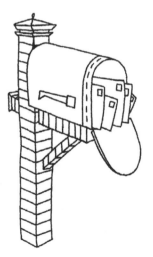

Find out when they will let you know for sure, and continue on with your production as if assuming you will be included (it would stink to find out you were in and then not have a lot of time to build up your inventory). You can also be in charge of your destiny here. If you don't want to be left hanging, perhaps only to eventually learn that a space didn't open up after all, you can get in touch with the event organizers and let them know that you would like to be removed from their waiting list.

Handling Rejection

Let's start with the worst-case scenario: You didn't make the cut. Okay, let's face it. Being rejected always sucks. You work hard, your stuff is made from pure awesome, and yet here you are being turned down by an event that felt perfect for you. You know your product would do well at the event; maybe you've even attended it as a customer yourself and saw lots of work that was comparable aesthetically and pricewise to what you do. You followed the guidelines to the letter, yet you were rejected anyway. It seems unfathomable!

First of all, it's normal to feel bad. Don't try too hard to talk yourself out of it for a while — but don't let it go on for too long. After all, it was just one fair (or maybe even a couple), and you know from your earlier research that loads of options are out there for you. Lots of people, including many prominent event organizers, will advise you not to take the rejection personally. Though that might seem like an odd statement — after all, your work *is* personal — after discussing this with many crafters, I've come to a few conclusions that might help you understand the acceptance vs. rejection process.

The first possibility is that a lot of people applied who do the same thing as you. This is very common when it comes to both knitting and jewelry. Fair organizers have to make sure they are offering a varied-enough selection of art and craft to keep shoppers interested. If the event is a general one, they need to have as many genres represented as possible. Naturally if the show is just jewelry, they can accept loads of jewelers, but at a general show, it just isn't possible to accept everyone who specializes in necklaces, no matter how fabulous all the necklace styles are.

Another possibility is that you could have done a better job with your application. Sure, you read everything and followed all the rules, but is it possible that you could have explained your work better or taken better photographs? Review what you turned in, and see if you can find anything you could improve on next time.

FROM THE CREATIVE COLLECTIVE: JENNIFER JUDD-MCGEE

I tend to sell a lot of prints of my artwork at fairs and typically offer some kind of special price that's cheaper than normal, which has been a decent marketing strategy for me so far. It's also fun to have something new at fairs that no one online has ever seen.

Ask a friend or two whose feedback you can trust to review your submission materials, and listen to what they have to say with an open mind.

Finally, if you still can't figure out why you were passed over, contact the organizers. Politely yet directly ask why you were rejected. If you send an e-mail, be sure to give them all the information they'll need to give you a quick critique without having to do the research themselves. Maybe include your artist's statement and your photographs in the body of your e-mail and ask them for some advice. Again, though, bear in mind that the people you're asking a favor from are very busy. Don't hassle them about it, and don't be aggressive or accuse them of rejecting you for no good reason. Chances are if you're up-front and polite and wait patiently, they'll get back to you with something helpful. Even if they tell you that too many people in your category applied rather than critiquing your work specifically, that is still valuable information. Conversely, you may not hear back from them at all, in which case just move on — and, again, try not to take it personally.

I've spoken with many people who run major craft fairs across the country and asked every one of them the same question: If someone is rejected by a fair, should they apply again to the same event in the future? Every single one of them said, "Absolutely." Keep that in mind, and know that not one person I talked to disliked anything that ever crossed their desk enough to not want to see it ever again. Most of the organizers I spoke with feel bad when they have to turn someone away, and many said they wish they could accept everyone who applies.

Preparing for the Fair

Now that we've dealt with rejection, let's consider the far more preferable option: You've been accepted! Good for you! Give yourself a big hug and toast your hard work. But then what?

The first thing to do is make a list of your inventory. Do you have enough of all your best-selling items? What exactly do you want to sell? Do you have a booth or table design already in mind? Are your tax licenses and the other official paperwork required by your state and the event in order? Preparing your items to sell in person can be a bit different than selling them online. Here are some tips to help you get started.

Products and Marketing Materials

Make sure all the little details of your products have been attended to, and everything you're planning on selling is ready to be sold. Some things are givens, whether the venue is your online store or an in-person one, such as making sure the loose threads are cut off of your fabric items, all of your prints are signed, or all of your cards and prints are packaged properly. But some differences exist between a virtual selling site and a real one. For example, make sure you have prices on everything, or at the very least, easy-to-read signs that clearly state the prices of your items. If you sell jewelry, do you have what you need to assist your customers, like a mirror for people to use when they try items on? And if you allow people to try on your earrings, do you have something to sanitize them with afterward?

Not only will you be selling your crafts or art in person, but you'll also be selling yourself. Bring your best marketing materials with you for people to take home with them, whether or not they buy something. Your table is a great place to have your business cards, promotional postcards, mailing list, and any other marketing tools.

Money Matters

Make a list of what you need to conduct your sales. Think about how you'll accept payment from people. You'll need a bank and a place to keep it. If you take credit cards, you'll need all the accoutrements of what that entails. I highly recommend you bring a receipt book in case anyone requests one. Also, have a complete inventory list of what you're bringing. If you don't offer customers receipts, you can use this list to keep track of what you're selling and for how much. Plus this sheet will come in handy if you use it after each sale to make note of what people buy. You may be able to spot some trends when the fair is over, such as a preference to buy a necklace and matching earrings set, or both prints and cards of the same design being purchased simultaneously. This information will come in handy when designing future products.

If both you and a friend are going to be in the same craft fair, share a postcard. You each print one side and have a stack of the cards at each booth. This way your pal's customers can learn about you, and your customers can learn about your friend.

Figure out how much your bank should be, and get it ready beforehand. If your items not rounded to the nearest dollar — say, $3.50 for a card — make sure that you have the wherewithal to make change. If you are charging tax on your items, try to work it out so that the tax is included in your price. For the most part at craft fairs people expect to pay what you say the item costs. If you charge $3.50 for a card and you need to add 25¢ tax, consider charging $3.75 instead. If the card says $3.50, and you ask your customer to hand over $3.75, it could be a bit awkward. Not because

people will balk at paying the extra two bits, but because you'll find yourself saying over and over again, "There's a tax."

Consider taking credit cards. (You can learn a bit about credit-card machines in chapter 3.) Lots of people come with just cold, hard cash in their hands, determined to spend only what they brought. But then, they hadn't counted on seeing that embroidered masterpiece portrait of Morrissey that you made, and now they just *have* to have it. Thank goodness you take credit cards.

Set-up Logistics

Scout out the venue location beforehand. Check the parking situation. Figure out where you'll load in and out. And while on the subject of loading, the way you pack your items in your car is also something to consider. Some people like to pack their products into their vehicle first and put in items like tables and chairs last. That way the display items come out of the car right away, so you can open up the table and have a place to set your products when you unload them. Figure out a system that works for you ahead of time. There is a good possibility that you'll already be slightly stressed out right before the big event, so make it easier on yourself by figuring out these small but important details ahead of time.

Designing Your Booth Space

How your space looks is super important, and designing the perfect booth or table can be a challenge. Not only do you need to consider what your booth looks like while actually standing in it but also how it looks from a distance. Investing in good booth or

table design is something that will pay for itself over and over again — and it's something that you won't have to make too many changes to for a while. In fact, keeping the look and design of your booth similar from show to show can help repeat customers find you.

Work out a plan ahead of time to make sure your booth is as functional and friendly and as cute as can be. Study other people's setups. If you can't actually attend multiple fairs to see who has done what (and what you should *not* do) this can easily be done online; there's even a Flickr group dedicated to show booth and table design. Consider having a few props to style your table with. Cute baskets

It's important to plan out how you're going to set up your booth before you get to the event. You'd be surprised at how tricky it is. Overall I'd say just experiment with it on your kitchen table, and put yourself in the customer's shoes and ask yourself if you'd be enticed to buy what you see.

to hold things, a clean, ironed length of fabric to cover your table — you get the idea. Make sure your space is accessible and your wares are easy for people to examine.

Booth Supplies

Pack up a box of miscellaneous supplies. I've included a list of the most useful items in the Resources section on page 214, but by all means add other things to it as you see fit. Also, check with any friends who are old hands at doing shows, and ask them what items they wish they had brought at one point or another but forgot.

I'm sure some of the things on the list may sound wacky, but you may need many or most of them. For example, cleaning wipes are handy to wipe down your table and chairs. Tissues may come in handy if your only bathroom option is a port-a-potty that has been used all day long and is now out of toilet paper — and hand sanitizer is also for that port-a-potty. Rope or clothesline could be used to tie your stuff down or create a make-shift display on which you could hang your prints if you need to. The small table is for your bank, the credit-card machine, and your bottle of water; it's hard to have these things on the ground, and you'll need all available display space to showcase your wares.

Fair Day Etiquette

Now you're finally there. You've set up your table or booth. It looks adorable! You have money needed to make change, you have promotional items to hand out, and your wares look great. You have really outdone yourself here. Oh! Here come the shoppers! They look excited. They're coming near your booth . . . they look at you . . . at your goods . . . and they walk on by. Hey, wait! What's going on here? Relax. Being passed by is part of the experience.

You need to put your show face on. Craft fairs are personal endeavors. Think about your customers and why they are shopping at a craft fair when they could be at the mall. They are looking for quality *handmade* items. They want something different, something unique. They are buying from you, not from a big-box store, so try not to present yourself as an employee at a big-box store. Be open and friendly. Smile at everyone who looks your way. Tell the people browsing in your booth a story about the item they're looking at. Engage them. Sell them more than a crocheted hat; sell them on your choice of orange and brown yarn.

Tell Stories

Pretty much everything you've done has a story of some kind behind it, and people want to hear it so make sure you tell them. Explain how the inspiration behind your color choice was the view of the park in your town during autumn. Or maybe your childhood kitchen was orange and brown, and your kitchen memory equates to "cozy." Make the personal aspect a part of the handcrafted experience.

People like to buy stories. It adds value to their purchase. They like to retell these stories, too. If you share the story behind what you made with your customer, chances are that when someone compliments them on their new hat, they will retell why you chose the colors you did. For more proof that this strategy works, take a look around at the handmade items you yourself have bought in person. No doubt you know some kind of story about them.

Look Welcoming

Stand up in your space, and look ready to interact with people. If rather than looking potential customers in the eye, you are sitting behind your table and chatting with your friend who came with you to help, it will seem like you're more interested in your friend than your patrons. And if you are not interested in them, obviously they will have little incentive to be interested in you or your wares. I know you'll be tired sometimes. Chances are you've been up for hours and have already done some hard physical labor. Maybe you haven't had the chance to eat breakfast yet, or quite possibly breakfast for you was hours ago and you never got lunch. Yes, you may be hot and tired and hungry, and chatting with your friend may feel like the only break you've gotten all day, but every time someone walks into your space, you have an obligation to dazzle them. Turn on your charm, you fabulous crafter you, and make a *new* friend.

Start Conversations

If you happen to get a lot of browsers to your booth or table and you're pretty sure they're not going to buy anything, don't stress about it. See it as an opportunity to sell them something in the future. Have them sign your mailing list, and give them a business card or a postcard with your booth number on it so they can easily find you at the end of the day in case they want to stop back. Work with them however they want to work with you. If you sell items (like hand-carved children's toys) for an audience that may not be your typical buyer, make sure you educate people as to how the items will work for them. Ask them personal questions such as, "Do you have any little boys in your life? A son? A nephew? A godson? Younger boys really respond to my hand-carved jungle animals!" You know: Schmooze.

Give Thanks

When someone does buy something, thank them genuinely. Smile, smile, smile. Say something sweet, like you know they'll really enjoy what they bought or that the blue of the silk-screened T-shirt is exactly the right color for them. You don't have to lie to people, certainly, and unless they tell you, you don't know if they're buying your crafts for themselves or as a gift. Just be genuine and interact. Think about how you like to be treated when you're buying something. Be your most authentic self when you're working directly with the public, and they'll respond to you.

FROM THE CREATIVE COLLECTIVE: MEGAN REARDON

When I go to craft fairs, I'm drawn to booths that clearly communicate what the maker is selling and look tidy and bright but also abundant.

Bring Along a Friendly Friend

On the other hand, let's face it: Not everybody who is creative is a people person. Some of us are just really shy, which is why we prefer working alone. Some of us have a hard time in crowds or speaking to strangers. If this is you, then you need a really strong Plan B: a super friend to help you. Find a friend (or family member) who is supportive, believes in you and your work, and would be willing to accompany you to the show. This person will be speaking for you and doing the whole engaging-the-customer thing on your behalf. They can be the

chatty one, allowing you to hang back, adding interesting tidbits here and there and answering direct questions. You can be the one to hand over the business cards and ring people up. If sales aren't your strong suit, you need to have someone with you whose strong suit it is. Also having a supportive friend with you will help when it comes to logistical problems like taking a bathroom break or getting a chance to see what other people are selling.

Starting Your Own Craft Fair

If there are no craft shows in your town, you might want to consider starting one. Make no mistake, organizing a show is hard work. It would be tough to do it all by yourself. You need to be into details and unafraid of dealing with people and numbers. If you feel like you're up to the challenge, though, by all means, move forward with the idea. Like any other big project you might take on, there are just as many rewards as there are challenges. Running an event can be a very satisfying experience, and to be able to create exactly what you're looking for yourself can be an exciting opportunity. Think of it! You'll get to meet so many people, further establish your crafty reputation in your community, and — bonus! —if you're in charge, you'll be sure to be accepted.

Gather a Group

If you decide that starting your own craft fair is just the kick in the pants your craft community needs, invite a bunch of like-minded folks to come together, and pitch your idea to them. This group will help you figure out if there is even interest in having a show locally. Your group can be made up of local shop owners who carry handmade items, other artists and crafters you know who live in your area, and anybody whom you think would have something to contribute to your overall idea.

Give them a fact sheet with the gist of your plan. Tell them how many vendors you think is a reasonable number and what venues you have in mind. The number of vendors you can host will be dependent on the space you book, which means you'll have to really scout out locations beforehand. Have a list of jobs you would need help with, and see if anyone assembled is interested in taking on these responsibilities. Propose dates to your group. Make sure you check national and local calendars when considering dates for your event. Obviously don't want to schedule your event at the same time as another big event in your (or a nearby) town or at the same time as a national show, which could draw your local people away.

Once you have a committee in place, an idea of where you want to host your event, and you've established that local vendors are interested in participating, you're pretty much all set.

Then you just need to do the work to make it happen.

More Tips for a Successful Show

1. If you can, wear or use something you're selling. If you sell seashell bracelets, wear them during the show. If you make silk-screened T-shirts, have one on. If you make wool hats and your show is in June, you may not want to wear a hat, but try to wear something else made from your signature wool collection — perhaps a knitted flower or maybe a knitted hip pouch for your money.

2. If you can be making something at the show, do so. I'm not suggesting the impractical, like taking your sewing machine with you, but you could be in your booth crocheting or embroidering or hand-stitching something. Get out your sketchpad, and work on designs for future projects. This provides a nice visual and says to your customers, "I am creative, and I'm happiest when I'm working." Plus it opens up conversation possibilities. People will remark on what you're doing, and it provides opportunities for you to tell those stories I talked about earlier. It doesn't have to be a big project or even something related to what you're selling — just something that displays your vision.

3. If you're showing at an outdoor event, find out ahead of time if dogs are allowed onsite. If so, consider having a water bowl at the edge of your space and bringing some dog biscuits. If nothing else, people with dogs will gratefully stop at your booth

so their pets can drink water, and you can strike up a conversation by asking if you can give their pooch a treat.

4. Think long and hard about playing music in your space. I know a lot of people like to have music around them at all times, and you may imagine yourself being sort of lonely and wanting music to keep you company. Hopefully, though, you'll be chatting it up with lots of people, and music may end up being a distraction. Also, why take the chance that not everyone will like your musical taste? Your items may be adorable but if you're blaring a style of music that turns someone off, chances are they'll walk right by. Also, imagine if your neighbor in the next booth was playing music you didn't like, and you were stuck beside them for a day or two. Wouldn't it get on your nerves? Probably, and you don't want to be that person.

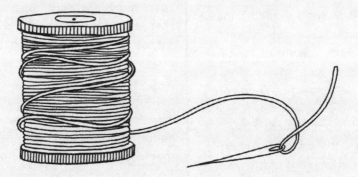

Alison Gordon of Boston Bazaar Bizarre

Proudly declaring that it's "not your granny's craft fair" on their website, Bazaar Bizarre began in 2001 in the Boston area as a hodgepodge of friends who organized their handcrafted DIY wares to both sell and entertain. In 2004 Bazaar Bizarre spread first to Los Angeles and Cleveland and then to San Francisco and San Mateo. For the past four years Alison Gordon has been a part of the committee that produces Boston Bazaar Bizarre. She also runs The Sampler.

What are the benefits of someone participating in a craft fair?

The best way to get people to buy your items is to get it in their hands. You can see things on the Internet, but you have no concept of the quality or time involved in making the item. It is just an image. When you get it in your hands, you can turn it around, see the construction, feel the materials. It's a completely different experience. As a crafter, you can talk directly to the shoppers and give them real-time answers to their questions and explain yourself to them. The interaction can help a lot of people through a sale. Handmade costs more, and some people need that little nudge to remind them that there's a person who spent 10 hours making that quilt, and this is how she supports herself.

There are also networking possibilities: chatting with other crafters about materials and construction, meeting with members of the press, finding new shops to carry your items — endless ways to further your business if that's something you are looking for. Some people use fairs as just a way to make a little money, but for others it is how they help to grow their business.

What helps someone get accepted to a big craft fair?

Experience really does help with getting into a big fair. I wouldn't suggest trying one out as your first fair; there just is no way to explain all the necessary preparation steps to someone who hasn't done any fairs. Plenty of small and midsized alt/indie fairs are out there, and many of us sell things that also translate fine to church/community fairs, so don't count those out!

Being established on the Internet also shows that you are prepared for a large volume of sales all at once. You don't even have to have your own shop, but showing that you are being carried at a significant number of Web (or brick-and-mortar) shops can prove that you are able to prepare for a large show.

The most important reason someone would get accepted to a fair, though, is quality. As I mentioned, seeing something in person gives a greater concept of the quality, which is why you often see the same vendors year after year at the big fairs. The organizers know their items and can count on them to be a great addition to the show.

Any tips for great ways to display awkward items like prints or stationery?

There are *lots* of great Flickr groups devoted to fairs and fair displays ("Show Me Your Booths" is the name of my favorite Flickr group for this purpose). At a fair, think height. Build a *stable* rack that can go high enough to show all your prints. If it fits in your product line, try to make it fun. One vendor created a cardboard house to display comics, and another makes little garden beds for her stuffed veggies. If you are doing a lot of fairs, invest the time into making quality displays. Peg-Board is your friend — add an easel, and you are set. Try to stick to a theme or color scheme to keep the displays from overtaking the booth.

What is the typical-size bank people should bring?

Ideally, you should have $250 in change for a large weekend show. This is for the worst-case scenario of the first few folks handing over a $100 bill for a $5 purchase. More realistically, for a big show, I would suggest at least $100: $40 in ones, $30 in fives, $30 in tens; for a small show, a conservative amount would be $50: $25 in ones, $25 in fives. A lot of people are totally broke right before a show; I know I've done shows with nothing, completely relying on neighbors to help make change, so don't let that hold you back at all. If all you have is $10, get it made into ones, and hit the show. Just do whatever you can; you'll make it through.

Any other good advice about craft fairs you can offer?

For a first fair — or for your first few, until you get an idea of how much you will sell — set up the fair space in your house somewhere. As you make things, work on a display, and lay it out as you go along. Make enough stuff to fill your entire space/table at least two times so as you sell things, you can replace them. Never put everything out, even if you think it doesn't look cramped. As soon as you start to sell, you'll just get emptier and emptier if you have no stock to replenish from. And try to create some cheap items; that helps to draw in shoppers. I get more $40 sales from someone who stopped to buy a $1 pin than I can count!

Chapter 10

SELLING IN ONLINE STORES

The easiest way to sell your crafts online is by taking advantage of one of the many online marketplaces for selling handmade goods. These types of online communities abound these days, and the most time-consuming aspect of this online entrepreneurial venture may well be researching the pros and cons of the various options. However, after you find the one that feels like home to you, setting up shop will be a walk in the park.

Evaluating Marketplaces

Deciding which is the right online marketplace for you can be tough, and you may be tempted to open more than one shop. (Check the Resources section at the back of this book for a list of the major marketplaces.) A good way to start is to spend some time poking around the forums of each site, finding out what other sellers are saying, and making a list of the pros and cons you see for each site. What does each site excel at? What are their general price points for what you make? The competition may vary from site to site, and what your competitors are able to sell their goods for is a really good indicator of whether or not you'll find success there. For example, if you want to sell prints of your illustrations for $25 each, but the top 10 sellers on the site you're considering seem to find success selling similar work but for much less, maybe it isn't the right place for you.

As you're reviewing your options, take note of a few important facts about each venue:

» How much of a cut does the site take from your sale?

» What kind of payment options do they allow you to accept?

» What is their traffic like?

» What will your competition be like?

» How is the site designed? Does it appeal to your personal aesthetic?

» What kind of reputation does it have?

» Are the site's current sellers happy with the service they're getting?

» What do the shops look like? Can you customize your shop how you want?

» What are the site's policies and terms of service? Do you understand everything you're reading?

The online venues I'm aware of have some major features in common: All of them will allow you to have an online profile and photos of your crafts, all of them need you to write descriptions of your items, and all of them let you set your own shop policies. The setup is simple: Once you've found a place you like, you can immediately set up shop. The converse benefit to these online marketplaces is that you can leave whenever you want. If you feel your sales are too slow or maybe you think your customers are shopping at other sites, you can simply pack up your virtual shop and move it elsewhere.

Setting Up Your Online Shop

How do you want your shop to look? The look of your online store should tie into your overall branding. (Read up more about branding in chapter 2.) Your branding will expand into your shop banner, the way you write your descriptions, and the way you interact with your customers.

Making a banner for your shop won't be too difficult. The online site where you're choosing to sell will give you the specific dimensions for how long and wide your banner can be. You should be able to easily make one with any photo-editing software you already have.

You'll also need to choose an avatar for yourself, and write up an "about me" section and a section defining your shop policies. The "about me" can be kind of tough for some people because it means talking about yourself. But here's the good news: You don't have to write about *yourself*, you need to write about your *creations*! Tell people what kind of materials you use, what inspires you, or what motivates you to be creative to begin with.

Defining Shop Policies

Your shop policies are a simple statement about how you do business. Pretty much anything your customer needs to know about buying from you should be here. Do you ship out within three days after an order is completed? Or do you save up your orders all week and go to the post office only on Saturday? Perhaps you require your buyers to purchase insurance. Maybe you only accept returns within five days — or maybe you won't accept returns at all. You may only take credit cards online via an online credit-card service. This is how you want to conduct business, and the policy section of your online store is where you inform your customers of your preferences.

Take a close look at the websites you frequent as a customer and at the stores you shop at in person. Chances are you'll find information on return policies clearly stated — either on a page link at the online store or on your receipt or located on a sign behind the counter of your favorite shop. Whether or not you routinely notice these details, these notifications are how businesses communicate their practices and policies with you.

Writing Product Descriptions

One of the few drawbacks to selling online is that people can't touch or smell or try on your product in deciding if they want to buy. They can only use their sight, so you need to give them all that you've got. Your descriptions should include every detail about what you're selling. Materials

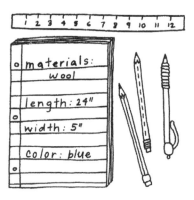

used, measurements, and anything else your customer would need or want to know.

People have all kinds of allergies — to synthetic fabrics, to natural fibers, to certain metals. Some people can't abide strong smells, and some people have reactions to certain kinds of glues. It is very important for people to understand what they are buying, especially when an item is handmade.

How you choose to write your descriptions is a purely personal decision — your own style will come through. You may be a witty writer, or you may be a just-the-facts kind of person. Whatever the case may be, be sure you are thorough.

Imagine you are your own customer. What do you need to know about something before you buy it? Do you want to know if the knit hat you are considering buying is soft? Scratchy? Is it big enough to accommodate your dreadlocks? Are those earrings big? How big? Bigger than the largest pair you own and are comfortable wearing? If you put yourself in your buyers' shoes and answer all the questions you would have yourself, you should be covered.

If you are selling wearables, tell people how you determined your measurements. Did you lay the garment down flat and measure just one side? If so, your customer needs to understand that they need to double the measurement you provided.

Another way to sell someone on your craft is to show them what they're getting in a very specific way — which means supplying nicely detailed photos.

Taking Product Photos

Now, naturally you are going to have pictures of your product. That's a given, but what are your photos saying about what you've made? The old expression "a picture is worth a thousand words" is still around for a reason, and you need your photos to get as close to a thousand words as possible. Most online stores let you post at least four photos of your item, and you should take advantage of the maximum they allow.

Take a look at your competitors' photos. What do you think works or doesn't work? What do you like or dislike? Use this information to help improve your own style. There are lots of ways to improve your photos even if you're not a professional photographer. I go into more detail about taking photographs in chapter 4; for now, I'll just talk about how to help your photos stand out in your descriptions.

Nothing helps people imagine something in their own life like seeing it in action.

PHOTO STYLING TIPS

Show your crafts in their natural environment. By that I mean style your photographs to give people a sense of what your wares may look like in their own homes. Maybe you make bookends. Display them in action, holding favorite books straight and tall on an attractive shelf. If you make vases, show your vase filled with a lovely wildflower bouquet.

Offer size references. I see this most with jewelry sales. A crafter of beautiful earrings states the dimensions and measurements. While that information is necessary and valuable, unless the customer has a mirror and a ruler handy next to their computer monitor, that good information won't be very useful. So photograph your amazing creations alongside something else for size comparison. Place a coin (or even a common item like an Oreo cookie or a Ritz cracker) beside your earrings to help patrons better determine the actual size.

USE MODELS

The best way to sell jewelry is by displaying it on an actual person. Telling a potential customer that the necklace she has her eye on comes on a 16-inch chain may not be as helpful as her being able to see where it falls on someone's neck. Ditto for earrings. If you sell dangly earrings, showing those beauties hanging from a pair of lobes is an image that can't be beat. Think about it: The only way for a customer to know if the length is right for her is to either measure all the earrings they already own or to craft a likeness out of string or paper and hold it up to her own ears in the mirror. So seeing those earrings in action, as it were, is a fabulous selling tool.

People are concerned about germs. If you choose to photograph your earrings in actual ears, and I hope you do, make sure to put a note in the descriptions telling people that you sanitize all your creations before shipping them and let people know how to sanitize them at home.

If you make clothes, display them on a body. Consider making a drawing of a body like you see in catalogs, and show people where you consider the waist, hips, and bust to be. This will help people take their own measurements. If you say a skirt falls just below the knee, designate exactly where that point is to you. It could be one inch below or maybe three. Since this would also vary depending on someone's height (that one-inch-below-the-knee measurement would be quite different on a 5'6" woman than on a woman who's barely 5 feet tall) exact length measurements of skirts, pants, and even tops is very important. The object is for your customers to really be able to tell if what you're selling is right for them.

Tagging Your Crafts

Tagging is pretty common these days: you tag photos of your friends on Facebook, you tag your photos in your Flickr stream, so chances are you know what it's about. Tagging your crafts in your online shop is especially important. It will help people find your store and your items. A tag is simply an explanatory word or keyword that helps shoppers find what they are looking for. Look through the description of what you wrote to help you figure out what your tags should be: item name, color, materials used, and any other descriptor to assist in leading customers to your product. Any word that is a selling point should be one of your tags. You may want to check out how your competition is tagging their items and then look at how your tagging compares.

You don't have to use obvious words in your tags, especially if they appear in your title. For example, you wouldn't need to use the word "handmade" as one of your tags because you are selling your item on a website that specializes in handmade items.

Here is an example of tagging that I took from a general item from Megan Risley's Etsy store. Megan sells hand-sewn items, and she has a lot of competition — but she does a really good job of tagging her crafts. One of Megan's specialties is quilts. A baby quilt she is offering in her store has been tagged with the following: *Quilt, patchwork, quilted, throw, coverlet, nctriangle team* (her local street team name), *lap blanket, baby quilt, pink, stripes, hot pink, baby, quilts,* and *blanket.* Typing a search of any combination of these words will bring up Megan's baby quilt listing: *pink quilt* or *pink blanket* or *baby blanket* or *hot pink stripes.* Megan also included the tag for the Etsy Street Team she belongs to, which will help people searching for something regional.

Living the Dream

Crafting full-time is the ultimate goal of many artisans — a goal that many in the Creative Collective have achieved.

I love making and selling things! This is what I've always wanted to do. I'm living my dream and giving others a little bit of happiness with each thing I make. That's just bliss.
— LIZ SMITH

Working without a boss to answer to is a blessing, but it also creates difficulty when you are only accountable to yourself. I find that I let myself off the hook for things I would demand from an employee, and I'm working to change this.
— LAURIE COYLE

When I can look at something and say, "I did that! I made that!" it gives me a big sense of accomplishment.
— AMBER KARNES

I'm able to do a lot because I have a very supportive husband, and I don't sleep much. I often stay up until the wee hours making a new apron to wear for a TV segment, working on an art quilt, writing a column, or editing a podcast. I like to be constantly working on projects, and I'm willing to do what it takes to get them done.
— JENNIFER ACKERMAN-HAYWOOD

Customer Service

Customers. You can't have a business without them. The care and feeding of excellent customer service relationships is pretty easy and can be a pleasure instead of the chore you might fear it to be. Above all, always putting yourself in a customer's shoes will have you well on your way to ensuring a repeat customer experience.

We all know the cornerstone for any good relationship, personal or business, is communication. No one likes to be ignored or left in the dark — especially when it comes to spending money. Even though you have built your business on handmade items, lessons can be learned from bigger retail operations.

Think about the types of purchases you make online. For example, when you order from a company like Amazon.com, you immediately get a confirmation e-mail telling you that your order has been received, processed, and what its estimated delivery date is. Once your order ships, you get another e-mail giving you the tracking number and some extra information, such as an invoice of what you ordered and a breakdown of how much you spent. A few days after your package arrives, you may also get yet another e-mail asking you to leave a review of the products you ordered and provide feedback on the service you received.

As a customer you have been involved in every single step of the ordering process, even the parts that are out of your control. The business has kept you in the loop, armed you with all the information you need about your purchase, and has provided what you need in case you encountered a problem.

Ensure Clear Communication

How should you communicate with your online customers? The conversation starts with your online presence. If you sell directly from your own website or use one of the many sites that allow you to have a Web store, make sure your message to potential buyers is clear, detailed, and in an obvious place. Welcome people to your site, and explain your shipping and return policies clearly. Shipping can be a bit tricky, depending on what service you use; you should be able to get a lot of information for your own policies from your carrier, especially since the shipping company, not you, sets those parameters.

Continue the conversation when someone places an order. Promptly send them a quick, friendly e-mail letting them know you have received their order and thanking them, and include useful information such as when you plan on sending the item out. Address them by name while you're at it.

Once you ship the package, send them another quick, personalized e-mail, and give them the tracking information if you use a service that offers that feature. Thank them again for ordering from you, and invite them to visit your shop again. You can also fit some sneaky marketing into this process by including links to other similar items in your shop or a link to your blog, or even asking if they would like to be added to your e-mail newsletter list. (See chapter 4 for details on marketing.) Try not to add images or any Flash to these e-mails as people may find that annoying, or they could take a long time to load and may not be seen.

If someone sends you an e-mail asking you a question or commenting on one of your handmade items, write them back straightaway. Quick, personal communication is key, and people appreciate it. Not only does it give your buyer or potential buyer confidence in you and your shop, but it also reflects positively on you as an artisan and businessperson.

Be Good for Your Word

Make sure that the policies for your shop are honest and easy for you to follow through on. If you promise to ship a sold item within two business days, you must do so. If you only ship on Fridays, you must always ship on Fridays. People do not like to be kept waiting when they've ordered something. Remember: There is a face to your business, and that face is yours. While you can learn a lot from bigger business and corporations, keep in mind that one of the main reasons people shop for handmade products is because of the personal connection. You are a real person, and people expect you to stand by your word.

Basically, if your customers make good with a payment, you must, in turn, make good with your promises.

While we're on the topic of being honest and providing people with excellent customer service, consider your shipping fees. People can tell if you are inflating your shipping costs at their expense, and it may feel dishonest to some customers. So if you need to make a few extra bucks on what you're selling, consider raising the price of your wares rather than tacking on a "handling" charge.

Also, be up front about everything you're selling. Be honest about things like the materials you use, if you're behind on shipping an item, or if a custom-made item is taking longer than you expected. Straightforward communication with your customers is imperative, and generally speaking, once you've made that human-to-human connection, people will be willing to work with you if you're experiencing an unforeseen problem. Wouldn't you expect the same if you were buying a handmade item from an independent shop on the Internet?

You aim for repeat customers, and repeat customers often will refer others to you if you make excellent customer service a hallmark of your business. People share good and bad shopping experiences with their friends and family. It is to your benefit and the benefit of your brand to ensure that people have only positive things to say about you.

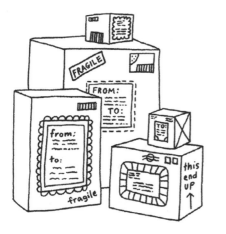

Go the Extra Mile

Consider how your handmade goods are presented when the box you packed is opened up. Would you rather open a box and find pretty tissue paper and ribbon lovingly wrapped around your new purchase with a sweet note attached? Or do you actually enjoy finding things shrink-wrapped inside those air bubble packs with an invoice? I myself would choose the prettier option every time, and most people who are choosing to buy handmade probably would, too. Of course if you need to use bubble wrap, you can always wrap tissue around it if you'd like — or, for that matter, wrap your fragile items with bubble wrap over which you use pretty paper.

Rarely do I get a package from a crafter that does not have a little something extra in it. I delight in those little giveaway buttons or postcards with artwork or a sample of a soap. You might want to think about adding similar items to your own packages along with a handwritten thank-you note. Even something short and snappy like, "Thanks for your order!" can often become a keepsake. It gives me a feeling of connection with the artist. I truly do save these things. The buttons and postcards get tacked to a bulletin board in my office, and I file away business cards that are some-times included with a note on the back of what I bought from the seller. When looking for gifts for special people in my life, I often go through these busi-ness cards and get new ideas and therefore place orders with people I've done business with before.

If you want to go the extra mile, consider following up with your cus-tomers. You could contact them and inquire as to how they are enjoying your handmade item, but be careful with follow-up. Some may consider receiving e-mails that they haven't initiated as spam. There are plenty of ways to continue a dialog with your customers if they are agreeable with-out coming off like a stalker. Do you have a business newsletter? If so, this is one way to keep in touch with your customers and encourage future sales. (See Create an Online Newsletter on page 99.)

Decide, too, if you want extras like delivery confirmation or insurance to be optional for your buyers. If so, consider what you would do if you sent an order out that was lost and uninsured or you sent an order to a customer and it was damaged in the mail through no fault of your own. Now your customer would like a refund for something that either didn't arrive or arrived damaged. What should you do? Respond quickly to their complaints, and ask them what they need to resolve the situation.

What you're striving for is to ensure that your first-time customers will be repeat customers. Providing the best customer service you can will take your business a long way toward achieving this goal.

Return Policies

The topic of returns can be a tough one. No one wants to work hard to create something, experience the joy of someone buying it, have the money added to your bank account, and then have the customer decide to return it. You and only you can determine your return policy, and as long as you stated it clearly, and the customer is aware of what your policy is before purchasing, you are covered in the event of a dispute.

·····• A True Story •·····

I bought an original painting from an online marketplace for my husband's birthday. It came all the way from England, and when it arrived it was damaged, and we were unable to frame it. As far as gifts go, it was a bust. I contacted the seller to let her know that her packaging was not sturdy enough and that the painting had arrived in an unacceptable condition. The seller wrote back immediately and offered me a new painting, which I accepted. The situation could have been avoided if she had packed the painting properly, and she accepted responsibility for that. As a result, she had to create another painting and cover the overseas postage herself. In the end, because she was gracious about it, I left her wonderful feedback.

Several things should be considered when drafting a return policy. To decide what will work for you and your handmade business, I suggest you do a little role-playing — with yourself.

SITUATION NUMBER ONE

Imagine you have been looking for a beautiful handmade hat to wear to work every day. It must match the winter coat you usually wear, it must fit well, and it must be of good quality so that you can wear it year after year. After much scouting around online, you finally find a hat that seems to fit the bill. The description says the hat is large in size (which is what you want to be able to fit over your hairdo) and gives measurements; the photograph shows the hat in the sunlight, and it is the perfect shade of green; plus it's in your price range. All the elements seem to be in place, so you decide to buy it.

When the hat arrives, it feels too tight. Also, the shade of green depicted in the photograph is different than the shade of green in person. You decide you would like your money back, and you contact the online shop where you bought it. They refuse to take it back, citing that their policies on returns are clearly stated on their website. How do you feel?

SITUATION NUMBER TWO

You are dreaming about a custom-made coffee table for your living

---

FROM THE CREATIVE COLLECTIVE: JENNIFER JUDD-MCGEE

I love that I make and sell things directly to people all over the world. I love being able to enclose a little note with something I made and have it go right from my hands into the recipient's. It feels kind of lovely and old-fashioned, even though it is only all possible thanks to high-powered new technology.

room. You research woodworkers and furniture makers and find one whose craftsmanship you like who says she can work within your budget. You decide to hire her, you draft plans for your new table, and you pay a deposit. When it's delivered, it is different than you imagined. The wood is the wrong color, and it is too big for the space. You refuse to take delivery and insist on getting your deposit money back. The woodworker denies your request, saying it is a one-of-a-kind piece made to your specifications, and while she won't charge you for the full amount, she is keeping your deposit. How do you feel as the customer? How would you want to be treated? Will you do business with this craftsperson again?

EVALUATING THE SITUATIONS

Let's rewind these two situations and have them play out differently. Say you contacted the hat maker, and she immediately agreed to refund your money (plus the return shipping cost) once she received the hat back. And what if the woodworker apologized and asked for a second chance to make the coffee table you wanted?

In this scenario, both sellers admit their mistakes and offer to resolve the problem in a way that is satisfactory to you. They respond promptly and keep in touch with you through the process. They have provided you with the best customer service possible under the circumstances.

Occasionally, of course, someone will want to return something or want a refund even when you are not at fault. If the package didn't arrive, don't burden your customer by telling them to take it up with your delivery service. Take it upon yourself to make things right, no matter what. It is perfectly acceptable to ask that someone wait a few more days for the package to arrive if you shipped it during a busy time of the year like the holidays, but be reasonable. If your customer is really freaking out, just find out what they need from you, and do it.

Small handmade businesses depend a lot on the connection to the customer. In the long run, it probably wouldn't be worth struggling and fighting with someone over money. All businesses take losses from time to time, and not everything always goes according to plan. Look for a solution that works for both of you. Perhaps your customer will accept another item in place of the one originally ordered. It's not uncommon to send a replacement and ask the buyer to return the original when or if it ever arrives.

If you refund a customer's money via a payment website like PayPal, remember that your customer is charged a fee on their end for accepting your refund, and to go the extra mile, you should consider calculating that when you refund them money.

UNSATISFIED CUSTOMERS

In a perfect world, everyone would be happy with you and your products all the time. You would always be paid promptly and always get rave reviews. Sometimes, though, things just don't work out. In this case you should:

- Try to remain upbeat. Use positive-sounding words when communicating with customers. Say, "What can I do to resolve this for you?" rather than "What do you want from me?"

- Try to find value in what your unhappy customer is saying to you. It could be that their complaint has some truth to it, which you may find helpful in the long run.

Answering Customer Questions and Comments

People like to ask questions. I know I do. In fact, usually before I click the Buy It Now button on an online store's site, I ask a question of the seller. Even though you can't look a potential buyer in the eye when selling online, you should respond to their questions or concerns immediately. Prompt, polite communication is very important, and it goes a long way with people.

Managing Feedback

Feedback is an essential part of your online business, and every selling site I know about has an option for people to leave reviews or comments about their purchases. Reviewing your feedback is another way a buyer may decide if they want to shop at your store or not. Hopefully people leave you glowing feedback all the time, mentioning your quick shipping, effective and safe packaging, and the overall incredibleness of your design, craftsmanship, and quality. They may just check off the positive option, though, and move on. No matter; as long as your can show that people dig your stuff and leave you good feedback, your rating should help ease the mind of new shoppers.

Are you getting some really great feedback about something in particular that you've made? Consider posting these compliments in the description of your item.

Just as you want your buyers to leave you wonderful feedback, they need the same from you. Take the time to leave feedback for everything you sell. What can you say about strangers? After all, you're not getting anything from them — other than their money. Well, what you do know is how they conduct business. Perhaps they paid you promptly. Or you can simply thank them for buying from you. A personal note in the feedback section is always appreciated and makes future buyers happy. Everyone loves compliments, so adding a small note

acknowledging that someone paid promptly and thanking her for choosing you means a lot. Sure, you can just click the "positive" button yourself and leave no extra kind words, but it can't hurt, right? You can wish her well or say something great about what she bought. This might attract potential buyers if they happen to be reading through someone else's feedback. Seeing something like: "Thanks for buying my button bouquet for your wedding! I hope you enjoy it!" may just make another browsing shopper curious enough to check out your shop.

Then there's the flip side: negative feedback. Negative feedback can happen to anyone for any reason. Yes, it will hurt and make you sad, but you need to learn to let it roll off your back. First of all, you're not happy with everything *you* buy, right? So it's going to occur with your goods as well. Someone may get something from you and not like it, and rather than e-mailing you directly and discussing his unsatisfactory (to him) experience, he simply leaves negative feedback. Depending on which site you're hosting your online store with, what you can do when you receive negative feedback depends on the tools they allow you to utilize. At some sites the feedback will be on your profile forever, while other sites offer a way for buyers and sellers to work out their problems and amend feedback.

No matter what, you need to remember that you are a professional. You are the seller, the creator, and you need to take the high road. Just because someone left you less-than-desirable feedback does not mean you should leave a nasty comment about your buyer in return. Best case scenario in this kind of situation is that your buyer contacts you with her issue *before* she leaves negative feedback for you. If she does, you have a chance to make it right.

Keep these customer service practices in mind at all times:

▶▶ The customers may not always be right, but they do deserve your full attention and respect regarding the matter at hand.

▶▶ Apologize first. What if you didn't do anything wrong? you may ask. Well, while that may be the case, that's not really the point. You can, in fact, regret that your customer is upset in any

regard. Simply recognizing that your buyer has a problem and has had to take the time out of a busy day to alert you to it is reason enough to apologize.

▶▶ Ask what will make the situation right. If what the customer wants is reasonable and you can do it, you should consider it.

▶▶ Taking a hit on a sale is a small price to pay when it comes to your overall reputation and the trust you are trying to build with your market.

RESPONDING TO POSTS ON OTHER SITES

Feedback can pop up anywhere these days. With all the social networking we do and all the places your business can appear online, finding comments about your work on other websites, like blogs or even your Facebook Fan Page, can happen. What if the impossible happens and you find something negative about your business? What should you do then?

Let's say someone out there has bought something from you and is not only unhappy but has used your Facebook business account to leave a less-than-stellar comment. While you could simply delete the comment and pretend it never happened, probably the best course of action would be to face it head on. Quickly post a reply that addresses the buyer's concern, and reiterate what you've already done to make things right (assuming you have), while also using it as an opportunity to point out the positive aspects of the product. Don't start an argument because that will merely aggravate the upset poster and make you look petty in front of your fans and potential buyers.

Consider this theoretical situation, where the upset poster never e-mailed you but instead chose to make his unhappiness into a potentially embarrassing public event by posting the following: "The blanket I got from Blankets A'Plenty is too thin, feels cheaply made, and doesn't keep me nearly warm enough."

If you were Blankets A'Plenty, a gracious reply post might be: "Hi, Poster! I'm sorry you're unhappy with the lightweight spring blanket you ordered. While it is a great three-season blanket, it might not be heavy enough to keep you toasty in the colder months. I use only the finest handpicked recycled materials in my blankets, and I can assure you the quality is top-notch. Perhaps you were looking for something with a little more "oomph," like my heavyweight winter blanket made from alpaca wool. If you'd like to exchange it, please send me an e-mail, and I'll take care of you right away."

Your quick reply tells them you are committed to making the customer happy. It also helps to educate the cranky buyer (as well as anyone else who might come across the post) that the product wasn't cheaply made, that the one she purchased wasn't made for winter use. You also appear helpful in making an enticing suggestion that might be a better fit for her needs, and you wrap up the post by directing her to contact you in a more private setting where you'll quickly work to make her happy. You come out smelling like a rose compared to Ms. Crankypants.

Alison Gordon of The Sampler shares a few behind-the-scenes marketing ideas.

First of all, what is The Sampler?

The Sampler is a marketing and promotional tool for indie businesses. Each month, independent crafters, artists, shops, zines, and record labels that run Web-based businesses send samples and promotional materials to a contribution pool. All the samples received are photographed, posted to the site, and then portioned out, put in little packages and sent off to Sampler subscribers, other Sampler contributors, and members of the media all over the world.

Is this the kind of thing someone trying to get exposure should look into?

The Sampler is great for two different types of crafters:

➡ People who are looking to get their items out to a large group of shoppers who are interested in crafts.

➡ People who are looking for media exposure (not everyone is). The Sampler gets sent to 40 different members of the media, publishers, bloggers . . . all sorts of people who can help your business take off.

Like a craft fair, The Sampler helps to get your actual work into the hands of potential shoppers. Not just any shoppers either; it's a prequalified group that is interested in hand-made, well-made crafts. Instead of sifting through pages of websites, they are instead sifting through a box of handmade items. They can see exactly what you make, how it is made, the care you put into the packaging . . . all the things that help a shopper make the leap to buyer.

190

Chapter 11

SELLING IN BRICK-AND-MORTAR STORES

Getting your handmade items into shops or boutiques may be easier than you think, and you don't have to go to the big gift shows to do it. But it does require some work. It means taking off your shy pants, if that's your usual mode of dress, and putting on your game face. You need to prepare yourself for the wide world of selling wholesale and meeting with shopkeepers. And, you will need to do some homework so that you know what shops you want to sell to and who you need to talk to.

Getting Your Foot in the Door

Let's start with the basics. Where do you want to sell your crafts? Start compiling lists of locally owned stores in your area that are good matches for what you make. Investigate gift stores, art galleries that have small shops within them, and even bookstores or cafés in your town that may sell related items to their customers; you don't have to confine your search to regular types of stores or boutiques.

Now that you have in mind some places to approach, take note of how close they are to one another; then rate the stores in the order in which you would most like to sell. The reason for that is most stores will not want to carry the same product as the store across the street or even down the road — in some cases a shop may even ask to be your exclusive retailer. Everybody wants their products or store to be unique, and the reason you shop at different stores even for the same kind of items like shoes is because different stores offer you different options.

It is important to be up front with the stores you're selling to. Let them know where else you will be selling your wares locally.

If possible, visit the stores beforehand. Knowing who the target clientele of the store is can help you better pitch your items. (You'd likely have a hard time selling tea cozies in a funky boutique in a big college town, but those tea cozies might be a huge hit a few towns over with a popular teahouse where the locals hang out.)

When you're researching, study up on the stores. Do they have a website where they feature what they sell? Do they have trunk shows? Do they sell similar products already? Make notes of these kinds of facts. It can help you narrow down your search.

Now that you know which stores you want to work with, and you also know all about them and are confident they are a good match, get down to the business of getting them to stock your handmade goodness.

Persuasive Leave-Behind Materials

When you go a-callin' on the shops, bring some of your marketing materials with you to leave behind. A shop owner may not want to write an order on the spot and may need some time to think about it. At the very least you should be able to leave him with excellent photos of your work, a line sheet and a fact sheet, and your business card.

Before you leave on your account-day marathon, make sure you dress for success. Be your own best advertisement by wearing your own jewelry or handmade clothes. If you don't make anything wearable, bring samples of your work with you. Nothing compares to being able to actually hold and handle something to see firsthand how it's constructed and what it's made of.

If you have a catalog or can make one, now would be a good time for you to employ it. However, if you're a smaller business than that, a modified version of a press kit will do. The photos should be of the same items you are hoping to sell in the shop, and the line sheet should have all the technical information that the shop owner will need to decide if she wants to carry your product. The line sheet will also tell her what your order minimum is, what your wholesale costs are for each item, and your return policy. The fact sheet could have your biography and a bit about your business, maybe some interesting tidbits about what you make that the shop owner could share with her customers. Leave your card to put in a Rolodex. And as always, make sure that every bit of

your contact information is on each piece of paper you leave behind.

Call ahead to make an appointment with the owner or manager at the shop you want to approach. You never want to drop in unannounced.

A drop-in sales visit can be awkward, especially if the owner or the manager is in the store alone; he might not have time to sit and discuss your line. If while you're browsing around town you happen on a shop that seems right for you, take the shop's card, and call to speak with the owner when you get home.

······ Things to Know ······
Before Approaching a Retail Store

Be prepared: Know everything about a store before you walk in. Beyond that:

➤ The shop may want you to set up your own display or want you to tell them how to best display your products. Have something in mind in case this comes up during your initial talks.

➤ Have your wholesale rate as well as your return policy figured out.

➤ Have an easy way for retailers to order from you, either at a special wholesale area on your website or an easy-to-use order form that you can leave with them. The easier you make it for the stores, the more likely they'll order from you.

➤ Map out a route of the shops you're planning on soliciting. If one store rejects you because they already carry a similar product, try the next store on your list. Just keep going.

Meeting with the Store Owner/ Manager

Shopkeepers and managers will want to know up front the basics: how much your items will cost them at wholesale, what kind of discounts (if any) you offer in quantity, where else you're selling, and, most importantly, how well your products sell. You need to have clear, concise, and (hopefully) profitable answers to those questions because if the owner or manager doesn't think your items will be big sellers, she's not going to devote floor space to something risky.

But this isn't a one-way street. You don't want to get your things into a store only to find out that it's not a good match for you. Don't be afraid to ask a lot of questions. How much room will be devoted to your product? Where will it be placed in the store? Do they carry anything that could be competition? Do they do a big mail-order or online business? How well is the store doing? They won't sit down and show you their books, but finding out a general, "Business is good!" or "We're going to close in a month because business is so bad" are good things to know.

Use this important time with the owner or manager to really connect with him. Some of the most successful companies have traveling sales reps who visit the stores that carry their products personally because it creates the kind of face-to-face connection that builds relationships. When you've got a good working relationship with a store, it'll be worth more than gold to you because they'll be a lot more likely to order from you than from a competitor. They'll also let you know what's going on with other stores in the area. Plus, if you have a good rapport with a shopkeeper, you'll be in a good position to respond to her needs quickly if some of your products aren't selling well enough (which gives you a good opportunity to suggest other things you make that might sell better), or if she keeps selling out of other items.

Geographically, you will want to keep the stores that carry your items at least a few towns apart if you're in a rural or suburban area, or limited to just a few locations in a major city. You might think that getting the most number of stores possible would be best, but then you'd run into a situation where your product has oversaturated the market. If someone walks into the first store and passes by your things, they'd most likely walk past them again in the next store as well. Not to mention, shop owners don't want to carry something that their competition down the street also has. Instead, they're going to want to carry a newer and more original product that would make their store stand out.

One thing to discuss with the owner or manager is cross-promotion. An easy and free way to promote each other would be to have an area on your website that says, "Available at the following stores . . . ." If this is your first store, you can say, "Available exclusively at XYZ Shop." In turn, ask the owner or manager to state on his website that he carries your products.

Just like magazines, most stores prepare for the holidays a long way out. (In fact, if a shopkeeper visits

FROM THE CREATIVE COLLECTIVE: DIANE GILLELAND

Whatever your chosen crafts are, try to find as many different ways to earn income from them as possible. If you make handbags to sell at shows, for example, can you also sell handbag patterns online? Can you teach handbag-making classes? Can you also make wallets and wallet patterns? Can you offer handbag repairs? I try to maintain lots of different ways to earn my living because they all have their upturns and downturns. The more diversified you are, the less you'll suffer in lean times.

New York City's biannual International Gift Show in August, she will be bombarded with the December holiday season merchandise and will most likely be placing orders with the holidays in mind.) Plan ahead and approach her well in advance with your own holiday line. Let her know what you'll have available, like holiday decor items or even fuzzy scarves that she may want to stock. This way you can make sure she has room in both her shop and her budget to work with you.

And what if those products don't go over as well as you and the store owner had hoped? If a certain product, or even a whole line of products, isn't selling in his store, a shopkeeper may ask to return the unsold items. This should not be taken as a personal reflection on you or your crafts. Keep in mind that the owner was impressed enough with your things that he wanted to carry them in the first place. If you have accounts at several stores, this will not be such a huge blow to you, but if this was your only retail outlet, it could definitely hurt. This is one reason why a good return policy is a must. If a shop buys from you outright,

returns shouldn't really be something you ever have to deal with. However, in today's economy, stores may want an insurance policy before they take a chance on a new line. If you *are* willing to take the risk of having product returned to you, which means you would have to give money back, consider charging a restocking fee. Just make sure that you are clear about your policies when you begin your business relationships. This will help you avoid embarrassing confusion later on.

Selling on Consignment

Selling your crafts at stores can sometimes be done by selling on consignment instead of wholesale. This simply means that a store will carry your goods, but rather than buying them from you outright, they take a percentage of the sale when your items sell. Assuming you can come to a mutual agreement of how much the percentage should be, this can benefit both the shop and you. A consignment split can be anywhere from 30/70 to 40/60 (which is the usual) to 50/50 (Be sure

Working with Terms

Let's say you've done your leg-work and lined up some retail stores to carry your goods. But although the shopkeepers want to order from you, they may not be able to pay right away. They may ask for "terms," which means that they order from you, you fulfill the order, and you invoice them later on. Typical terms are 30 days or 60 days. Some people will only set up terms after a store has ordered and paid promptly a few times. Or you may require a store to order more than your standard amount if they want terms.

There are pros and cons to accepting terms. On one hand, you may not be able to financially let your work go without immediate payment. If that's the case, explain that to the person placing the order and see if you can work something else out. On another hand, just because you accept a store's offer and you agree on when you'll get paid, even if you send an invoice, you may find yourself in the position of having to act as a bill collector if the store does not pay on time. You may want to ask the shop for references. Stores are used to having to supply references to larger vendors, so it shouldn't be a problem. It is a way that they can prove their credit worthiness.

The pros to accepting terms could be anything from reducing the inventory you have on hand (freeing up room for you to make more product), to endearing your-self and your line to another small business owner, who will appreciate your cutting her a break, therefore creating a repeat buyer.

Whatever you decide to do, just be clear about your expectations and get everything in writing.

you know which number represents you when agreeing to splits.). Also, some stores will charge you a monthly fee to be in their shop. For the fee, I've heard everything from 1 percent of your monthly sales to $20. (One of the biggest drawbacks to selling on consignment is the inevitable effect of breakage, theft, or wear and tear on your products.)

Remember, a shopkeeper isn't just pocketing all the money an item sells for. They need to pay their overhead — rent, electric, water, Internet and phone bills, insurance, and credit card fees — out of every sale.

So how does consignment work exactly? It's pretty simple. You find a shop you want to work with, and then you simply hammer out the details. Here are some questions to ask before settling on a store:

- ➤➤ Will they want you to create your own displays?
- ➤➤ Will they need you to tag your own items? If so, what information will they want?

- ➤➤ Where will your items be displayed?
- ➤➤ When do they send checks out?
- ➤➤ Do the consignment rates increase around holiday times?
- ➤➤ Does their insurance cover any possible theft or breakage of your wares?

Always check references for stores that you're considering. And I mean don't just ask the store or gallery owner to supply you with references, although you should do that, too. Check with other people who have worked with them. Also, do a thorough Internet search to make sure they are on the up-and-up and to see if they have had any reported problems working with crafters before. However, always ask the shopkeeper for his side of the story if you read something that causes you concern.

A final note: A lot of crafters report being approached by brick and mortar stores who want to sell the crafters' items on consignment. The buyers at these stores find items they want to sell via crafters' websites, blogs, and online shops, so keep that possibility in mind when you are designing them.

Jenny Ryan of Felt Club

Jenny is an all-around amazing crafter. Not only does she write for online publications like CRAFT *and* Apartment Therapy LA *and has published a craft book called* Sew Darn Cute: 30 Simple Projects to Sew and Embellish, *she also owns and teaches at Home Ec., a crafting workshop and retail space in Los Angeles. But that's not all! Jenny also founded and produces Felt Club, the largest indie craft show in Southern California.*

How did you come up with the concept of Felt Club?

Initially a friend and I envisioned Felt Club as an online crafting website with tutorials and articles. We came up with the name after seeing the movie Fight Club, of course, and thought it would be funny to put a spin on the whole "club" concept but in a crafty way. We bought the domain name and wrote a few articles. Unfortunately, life got in the way, and it just kind of went nowhere, and we never launched it. Several years later, after exhibiting at shows like Renegade and Bazaar Bizarre (the latter of which I helped organize), I tried to figure out a way to get my handmade goods seen on a more frequent basis than just once or twice a year. I also wanted to show off my wares in person and not just online. Many of my friends were in the same boat, so I started thinking about putting on my own show in LA. A local comic book shop expressed interest in hosting a handmade marketplace, so I [began] putting on monthly shows in their parking lot. Felt Club's first annual holiday event happened in 2006. From then on, I've concentrated on holding big shows once or twice a year. I've found (at least for the LA crowds) that the anticipation is higher if we hold larger shows less often rather than monthly.

If someone wanted to start a craft fair in his hometown, what advice could you give him?

Be sure you can commit to giving the show everything you've got. For a show to succeed, you need to treat it like a real job. It's not enough to gather some cool crafters in a room and hope people show up; you need to do everything you can to let people know about the show and to get people involved. Having a core group of dedicated and dependable volunteers is key.

What are the benefits of starting a craft fair of your own?

As a crafter myself, I've enjoyed the process of trying to create the kind of show I'd love to exhibit at. Coming up with new ways to make the show fresh and exciting every year is a fun, creative challenge.

What is the best thing about creating something like Felt Club?

Definitely the feedback from the community, by which I mean both the exhibitors and the visitors. The enthusiasm and loyalty shown by Felt Clubbers means the world to me. Every year I expect no one to show up, and every year the reaction is bigger and crazier and more heartfelt.

Chapter 12

GET CREATIVE
Other Selling Options
and Opportunities

You have an online shop, and you are all up on the various ways to sell your goods through consignment, wholesale, and craft fairs. What else could there possibly be? Let me tell you, my friend, there are many other creative ways you can get your products in front of people. Consider, too, that your crafty knowledge and your experience are just as valuable as what you make. When it comes to selling your work, think about branching out a bit.

Join a Co-op

Are there any art or craft collectives or co-ops in your area? These are member- or community-based organizations that usually have a brick-and-mortar space where the members sell their goods to the public. Members often pay a fee to belong and are sometimes required to chip in and help with such things as cleaning the space and staffing the shop.

The benefits to belonging to a group like this (or starting one!) are many. They usually advertise in local publications, have monthly show openings, and are able to build a regular walk-in customer base. It can also be a great way to rotate your work, get live feedback, and make new friends.

Teach a Course

Want to reach more potential customers? Teach a class! Chances are numerous people have asked you how you do what you do. Perhaps you should show them! Start feeling around to see who would be interested in learning your craft from you. Think up a course idea, write a description, figure out what to charge, find a space to host your class — your local library, community center, or even a neighborhood church may have space that you could use or rent for a reasonable price — advertise, and then begin to accept the people who sign up!

The beauty of teaching a course is that even if you are instructing people how to make something like what you sell, they'll likely come to realize what actually goes into your work and appreciate what you do all the more. Leading them to buy your wares, of course.

Hold Trunk Shows

Is there a boutique or store near you that sells items that are complementary to your style? Do any of your local customers have connections at a store where you'd like to sell your line? If a store you have your eye on doesn't do consignment, and you're not ready to sell wholesale (or the store doesn't want to take a chance on your product yet), ask about having a trunk show. If you make something that's a good match for a nearby store, having a trunk show is a great way to expose your work to local people who might not know about you.

A trunk show involves you and a shop owner choosing a date and a time where you will come into the store and set up a display of your wares. You will need to advertise ahead of time (leave professional promotional materials at the shop if the owner will allow it, notify your newsletter subscribers, place flyers at nearby coffee shops), and then show up well prepared.

If you make something wearable, try to arrange for the staff to model something you've brought to sell. And, of course, you, too, should wear something you've made yourself! The store you're working with will most likely take a cut of your sales, but it's still a win for you.

Host House Parties

Most of us have been invited to candle or kitchenware parties at one point or another. You know what I'm talking about. Your coworker's sister hosts a party, you go just to be supportive, and you come home with something you wouldn't have bought otherwise — like a hundred pineapple-scented tea light candles. While house parties are a lucrative idea — hey, Tupperware is a household name based on this selling concept — why not put a more modern spin on the idea, and throw a house party to sell your crafts?

Get a bunch of artisan friends together in one place, have them invite *their* friends, and put on a mini craft show. The fun combinations here are endless: crafts and potluck, a crafty picnic, a wine-and-yarn night . . . you could sell your work or trade supplies or exchange ideas. Maybe even try having a crafting demonstration at one of these events.

Take turns hosting them within your community, and see where it goes. Invite a local media person to write about them, or ask that shop owner you've been wanting to work with to attend. You may wind up with more than just sales!

Offer Kits and Patterns

Have you ever thought about selling kits or patterns? Can you compile kits for what you do or a similar idea for what you make? If so, try selling them! If you are an amazing seamstress and are known for creating fabulous one-of-a-kind replica vintage dresses that you can't seem to make fast enough to keep in stock, how about drafting up a pattern and selling it as an option for customers who are brazen enough to go it on their own? Selling patterns for your work is also a great way to vary your price point. If you sell a dress for $150, selling a pattern for a considerably lesser price is a great way to make money from the same product twice and from two different markets.

You can even sell your patterns as PDF files, which means less overhead for you. You simply design the pattern, create the PDF file, and post it in your online shop. Customers buy the PDF, and you e-mail it to them once the payment clears. Easy peasy!

Patterns and kits for things that are similar to what you're already selling are also a great way to expose people to what you do. If you don't want to give away your craft secrets, consider patterns or kits that complement your wares and will appeal to your existing customer base. You might even try having a monthly theme or devising special items for holidays.

Whatever you come up with, these offshoots may also be a great way to find new inspiration and creative direction for what you're doing.

Q&A WITH
Jennifer Ackerman-Haywood

Jennifer's popular craft-focused podcast and blog, CraftSanity, is well-known in crafting circles. Jennifer also writes a weekly craft column for her local paper and works with a local TV station demonstrating craft techniques on a news program.

What led you to podcasting?

I was on maternity leave from my newspaper job, and my husband, Jeff, was listening to a lot of tech podcasts. When I asked what a podcast was, he suggested that I produce one about crafts. I told him he was nuts, then got to work planning my first episode. I had no idea what I was doing and fumbled around for my first episodes. But now, after producing more than 100 shows, I feel like I'm getting the hang of it.

How did you decide to continue?

I started to get feedback from nice people around the globe who enjoyed the podcast and encouraged me to keep producing it. I also couldn't ignore how much fun I was having and how great I felt after recording an entertaining interview with a talented crafter.

How can podcasting help one's business?

Podcasting is a great way to build an audience for your product or brand. If people feel connected to you, then they're probably more likely to support your business.

How did you spread the word to get listeners?

I didn't take an aggressive approach to building an audience; I simply let it grow organically. All episodes of my show are available for free download on iTunes, so many people initially found my show by searching for craft podcasts there. As far as I can tell, most listeners have found CraftSanity through the many blogs that have mentioned the show since its humble beginning in 2006.

How do you decide what topics to cover in your podcast?

I enjoy all forms of art and craft, so for the most part this means *everything* is a show possibility. I try to time show topics with the release of interesting new books or other events that listeners can participate in.

What do you look for when scouting for guests?

Talented people with interesting stories. Many of the people I interview have books, but I love to interview artists and crafters on their way up, people who are making cool stuff but haven't told their story a million times. It's fun to "discover" people and then watch their stars rise.

Have you ever been approached by someone who wants to appear on your podcast? Are you open to that kind of communication from people?

I am approached frequently by people who want to be on my podcast, and I'm fine with that. I've interviewed several people who have approached me first. Most podcasters are open to being contacted by prospective guests, but do your homework before you fire off an e-mail. Listen to the show to familiarize yourself with it. And never gush about the show and say how much you love it when you've actually never taken the time to listen to it. It's annoying when people fib to try to get free publicity.

What advice would you give to a person who wanted to start podcasting?

Listen to other podcasts, and decide what kind of format you like. Do you want to be the only voice listeners hear? Or, do you want to produce an interview show? Once you decide on the format, make it your own. If you try to model your show after someone else's exactly, it probably won't be very good. Do what feels natural to you and that's what you'll do best.

PARTING ADVICE

Selling your crafts is an adventure. You get to not only be creative while actually crafting something with your hands, but what you choose to do with it afterward is a creative process, too. How you go about selling your wares will depend on what your goals are. It is important to remember that you don't have to quit your job if you want to make some side money; conversely, you don't have to craft on just a part-time basis if you're ready for something more.

Making things with your own two hands is satisfying on so many levels, and chances are when you first fell in love with polymer clay or a sewing machine or weaving rugs from old T-shirts, you loved it precisely because it made you feel good. Keep that perspective in mind when you're creating. The business side of your business should be just as much fun and just as rewarding. The other kind of rewarding. . . .

If You Could Only Give One Piece of Advice . . .

I've chosen to end this book with more great advice from my Creative Collective. I asked each one of them what one piece of advice they would give to a crafter that would apply at any point in their creative adventure. I think they sum up the ideas and concepts of *The Handmade Marketplace* beautifully. Herewith are my favorites for you. Enjoy, dear readers!

DIANE GILLELAND

I actually have two pieces of advice. The first one is to diversify all you can. Don't try to rely on one product or service for all your income. The economy is too volatile. Whatever kind of creative work you do, there's more than one way to earn money from it. Secondly, if there's something you dream about doing for a living, find a way to do it *right now*. By this I mean seek out some small way to engage in it without pay or for minimal pay — and not as a job working for someone else but as your own effort. I wanted to be in business for myself as a crafter for years, but nothing happened until I started putting myself out there via my blog and podcast. Those led to more opportunities and, more importantly, gently got me to begin embracing the role of entrepreneur.

LIZ SMITH

Don't worry about where you are in the process of building your business. Everyone is at a *different* stage, but everyone is at *some* stage. Listen to people ahead of you, help those who are still catching up to you, and don't be intimidated by people who seem to have it all figured out. No one has it *all* figured out.

AMBER KARNES

Have fun, do what makes *you* happy, and don't worry about trends or what others think.

TARA SWIGER

Decide what your end goal is! Want to craft for the fun of it? Then make what *you* want! Want to earn some money? Then figure out who your target market is, and focus on *them*.

PAUL LOWE

Be true to yourself. Do what you say you want to do, don't just talk about it.

MATI ROSE MCDONOUGH

Make a schedule and goals and re-evaluate on a weekly basis your progress and priorities.

LAURIE COYLE

Don't try too hard to force your style; it will come. Starting out, I really wanted to know what my work would eventually look like or what people would really respond to, but this has to come through trial and error. You try something, and [either] it works or doesn't. You can't get discouraged by the things that don't work; there is an audience for everything — and sometimes the trick is finding that right audience for your work!

JENNIFER JUDD-MCGEE

Love what you're making!

AMY KAROL

Just make yourself happy with what you do. Yes, that old cliché. But really, that's what matters. The rest will come together, and if it doesn't — so what? At least crafting makes you happy. Sometimes making money at something is what can kill it.

NICOLE VAUGHAN

Try! Have a go! Experiment! Most of all, have fun and enjoy it!

RESOURCES

Here are some general resources that will help you further explore the topics covered in *The Handmade Marketplace*. A copy of this list along with checklists, business forms, and other helpful information are maintained on my website, www.karichapin.com, and I encourage you to check in there occasionally for updates to these categories: I've seen some new websites come into the handmade scene since I began the writing of this book. I also welcome your additions. Any suggestions you may have can be sent to me at thehandmademarketplace@gmail.com.

My Creative Collective has provided me with endless inspiration, and I hope that you will take a closer look at each of their websites, which I know you'll enjoy. I would like to thank each and every one of them for the invaluable contributions they made to *The Handmade Marketplace*. If you were inspired or moved by anything you learned from them here, please let them know!

Creative Collective

Alison Gordon
www.sewmaryann.etsy.com

Amber Karnes
www.7citiescrafters.com

Amy Karol
www.angrychicken.typepad.com

Ashley Goldberg
www.ashleyganddrew.com

Betsy Cross
www.betsyandiya.com

Caroline Devoy
www.jcarolinecreative.com

Diane Gilleland
www.craftypod.com

Elizabeth MacCrellish
www.squamartworkshops.com

Emily Martin
www.theblackapple.net

Grace Bonney
www.designspongeonline.com

Holly Becker
www.decor8blog.com

Jen Skelley
http://jenskelley.com

Jennifer Ackerman-Haywood
www.craftsanity.com

Jennifer Judd-McGee
http://swallowfield.etsy.com

Jenny Ryan
www.homeecshop.com

Jessica Marshall Forbes and
Casey Forbes
www.ravelry.com

Karen Walrond
www.chookooloonks.com

Kim Werker
www.kimwerker.com

Laurie Coyle
www.lauriecoyledesigns.com

Leah Kramer
www.craftster.org

Liz Smith
http://madeinlowell.blogspot.com

Mati Rose McDonough
www.matirose.com

Matt Stinchcomb
www.etsy.com

Megan Reardon
www.notmartha.org

Megan Risley
www.megrnc.etsy.com

Natalie Zee Drieu
www.craftzine.com

Nicole Vaughan
www.craftapalooza.com

Paul Lowe
www.sweetpaul.typepad.com

Tara Swiger
www.blondechickenboutique.com

Yvonne Eijkenduijn
www.yvestown.com

Websites/Community/ Blogs for Crafty Businesses

Glitter
www.supernaturale.com/glitter/

Venus Zine's "Crafting a Business by Jenny Hart"
www.venuszine.com/users/JennyHart

The Switchboards
www.theswitchboards.com

The Storque (look for topics under the heading "Indiepreneur")
www.etsy.com/storque/

Craft Boom
www.sparkplugging.com/craft-boom/

Indie Biz Chicks
http://indiebizchicks.com/wp/

Design*Sponge Biz Ladies column
www.designspongeonline.com/
category/biz-ladies

Not Martha
www.notmartha.org
Technically this is not a business website per se, but Megan Reardon posts lots of excellent links and some of them are craft-business related.

Blog Hosting Options

www.blogspot.com
www.typepad.com
http://wordpress.org
www.moveabletype.org
www.squarespace.com

Legal and Government Resources

Official Business Link to the U.S. Government
www.business.gov

U.S. Small Business Administration
www.sba.gov

SCORE: Counselors to America's Small Business
www.score.org

Internal Revenue Service
www.irs.gov

Creative Commons
http://creativecommons.org
Not just for U.S. citizens
For lawyers in your state, simply Google your state + "Lawyers for the Arts"

General Crafting Podcasts

www.hellocraft.com
www.craftypod.com
www.craftcast.com
http://craftsanity.com

Primary Online Marketplaces

Etsy
www.etsy.com

Big Cartel
www.bigcartel.com

1000 Markets
www.1000markets.com

Supermarket
www.supermarkethq.com

Art Fire
www.artfire.com

International Online Marketplaces

Folksy
www.folksy.com

iCraft
http://icraft.ca

Craft Fetish
www.craftfetish.co.nz

DaWanda
http://en.dawanda.com

Made It
www.madeit.com.au

Craft Show Supplies Checklist

SETTING-UP-YOUR-BOOTH SUPPLIES
- ☐ Scissors
- ☐ Packing tape
- ☐ Rope or clothesline
- ☐ Clothespins
- ☐ Bulldog clips
- ☐ Large ziplock-style plastic bags
- ☐ Weights
- ☐ Your handmade goodness
- ☐ Table
- ☐ Chairs
- ☐ Banner
- ☐ Table covering
- ☐ Cushion for your chair

PERSONAL SUPPLIES
- ☐ Paper
- ☐ Sunscreen
- ☐ Water
- ☐ Packet of tissues
- ☐ Lip balm
- ☐ Hand sanitizer
- ☐ Camera
- ☐ Cleaning wipes
- ☐ Sunglasses
- ☐ Snacks

MAKING-A-SALE SUPPLIES
- ☐ Scotch tape
- ☐ Shopping bags
- ☐ Pens
- ☐ Bubble wrap or tissue paper
- ☐ Small table for credit-card machine
- ☐ Credit-card machine
- ☐ Change/bank
- ☐ Locking money box
- ☐ Hard surface for people to write on
- ☐ Colored dots
- ☐ Sales slips
- ☐ Business stamp
- ☐ Calculator
- ☐ Any required licenses
- ☐ Boxes, if you sell delicate things

MAKING-FUTURE-SALES SUPPLIES
- ☐ Mailing list sign-up sheet
- ☐ Promotional materials
- ☐ Business cards

GETTING-THERE SUPPLIES
- ☐ Map of the craft show
- ☐ Directions to show

INDEX

Accounting, 41–43, 54, 60
Ackerman-Haywood,
Jennifer, 7, 178,
206–207
advertising, 107–27
artist's statement, 152
attorneys, 38, 54, 213
auctions, 114
audience, 29, 119
audit, 62
avatars, 110, 134, 149

Badge, 112
balance sheet, 61
bank account, 42
banners, 90, 112, 173
Bazaar Bizarre, 168
Becker, Holly, 6, 101, 116,
125–27
Betsy & Iya Jewelry, 50–51
Black Apple, The, 30, 33
blog reader, 91
blogs, 84–106, 126, 212–13
ads on, 108–109
appearance of, 89–90
comments on, 96–98,
112
content for, 92–95

design of, 116
hosting services for, 213
links on, 111
micro, 132
and photographs, 95
promotion of, 95–96
and sales, 51
setup of, 87
style of, 88
success with, 98–99
traffic on, 92
writing a, 87–89
Bonney, Grace, 6, 81–83,
89, 100, 116
bookkeepers, 41–43, 54, 59
booths
craft fair, 150, 160–61,
169
Boston Bazaar Bizarre, 168
branding, 27–36, 122, 139,
173
business
cards, 65–66, 113
name, 32–35, 68–69
practices, 37–55

Camera, 16–17, 73–75
CAPTCHA, 97

categories, 91
checks, 44
Chookooloonks, 73
comments
blog, 96–98, 112
customer, 186–89
community, 3, 21, 67,
76–83, 104–106, 212
competition, 47–48
complaints, 187–89
consignment, 197, 199
contests, 95
cost of goods, 48
Coyle, Laurie, 8, 19, 101,
178, 210
craft cooperative, 203
craft fairs, 146–70
acceptance to, 169
applying to, 151–54
benefits of, 168
booths at, 150, 160–61,
169
customers at, 161–64
evaluating, 149–51
finding, 147–49
logistics for, 150–51,
159–60, 165

craft fairs (continued)
  and marketing materi-
    als, 158
  and money, 158–59, 170
  organizing, 164–65,
    200–201
  preparation for, 157–61
  rejection from, 155–57
  research about, 147–49
  supplies for, 150, 161,
    214
  timing of, 149
CraftyPod, 142
Creative Collective, 4–10,
  209–12
creative process, 19, 94
credit cards, 44–46
Cross, Betsy, 5, 50–51
cross promotion, 196
CSS, 91
customers
  communication with,
    179–82
  at craft fairs, 161–64
  feedback from, 186–89
  knowing your, 29
customer service, 67,
  179–89

Dashboard, 91
DBA, 35
decor8, 116, 125–27
deductions
  tax, 56–59
delivery confirmation,
  182–83
depreciation, 58
descriptions
  product, 174–75
  designer, 54, 90

Design*Sponge, 81–83,
  89, 116
Devoy, Caroline, 5, 56–62
direct message, 133
Doing Business As, 35
domain name, 34–35
donations, 114
Drieu, Natalie Zee, 9, 78,
  94, 120, 151

Eijkenduijn, Yvonne, 10,
  16, 23
e-mail, 102, 110, 117,
  178–81
Etsy, 67, 177

Facebook, 136–37
fact sheet, 121–22, 193
fairs. see craft fairs
Fan Page, 137
feedback, 157, 186–89
feed reader, 91
fees
  credit card, 45
  shipping, 181
Felt Club, 200–201
financial
  advice, 56–62
  records, 41–43
  statements, 61
Flickr, 138–41
flyers, 112–13
Forbes, Casey, 7, 104–106
Forbes, Jessica Marshall, 7,
  104–106
forums
  online, 110–11

Gilleland, Diane, 5, 130,
  142–44, 196, 209

giveaways, 95
goals, 15
Goldberg, Ashley, 5, 14
Gordon, Alison, 4, 168–70,
  190
guidelines
  craft fair vendor, 151–52
  submission, 116–17

Helpers, 53–55
hosting services
  for blogs, 213
  for podcasts, 130
house parties, 204
HTML, 91

Ideas, 24–25
identity, 28, 31, 36
income statement, 61
inspiration, 16–17, 20–25
insurance, 182–83
intern, 55
Internal Revenue Service,
  43, 60–61
interviews, 207
inventory, 59, 157–59, 170
iTunes, 144, 206

J. Caroline Creative, 56
Judd-McGee, Jennifer, 7,
  156, 184, 210

Karnes, Amber, 5, 22, 30,
  178, 210
Karol, Amy, 5, 14, 22, 100,
  210
kits, 205
Kramer, Leah, 8, 135, 160

Legal advice, 38, 54, 213

LibSyn, 130
lighting, 71, 74
Limited Liability Company
(LLC), 40
line sheet, 122, 193
links, 111
logistics
for craft fairs, 150–51,
159–60, 165
logo, 35–36
Lowe, Paul, 10, 70, 119, 210

MacCrellish, Elizabeth,
6, 26
magazines, 118–20
marketing, 64–75
and craft fairs, 158
creative, 114–15
firm, 54
materials, 65–75, 193–94
online, 129–44
mark up, 48–49
Martin, Emily, 6, 18, 30, 33
materials
cost of, 48
description of, 174
marketing, 65–75,
193–94
McDonough, Mati Rose, 8,
14, 23, 55, 78, 101, 210
media, 115–27
message board, 110–11
mileage, 56–67
models, 176
money
collecting, 44–46
and craft fairs, 158–59,
170
motivation, 12–15, 22–23

Name
business, 32–35, 68–69
national attention, 127
newsletters, 99, 102–103
newspapers, 118

Online
advertising, 108–12
community, 77, 104–106,
212
marketplaces, 213
media, 115–17
newsletters, 99, 102–103
presence, 84–106
stores, 171–90
order confirmation, 179

Packing
for shipping, 181–82
partnership, 39
patterns, 205
photographs, 70–75
and blogs, 95
for craft fair applica-
tions, 153–54
and Flickr, 138–41
importance of, 125–26
and marketing, 83
and models, 176
and press kits, 122
styling tips for, 175–77
PodBean, 130
podcasts, 129–31, 142–44,
213
and advertising, 109
publicizing of, 131,
206–207
sponsorship of, 109, 143
policies

return, 173–74, 183–86,
197
shop, 173–74
portfolio, 127, 153
postcards, 68, 159
press
kit, 82–83, 121–23, 126,
193–94
release, 123–24
pricing, 46–53
products
descriptions of, 174–75
trading, 113–14
promotion
cross, 196
promotional postcards, 68,
159
public
working with the,
161–64
publicity, 54, 107–27, 131

Queen Bee Creations,
113
QuickBooks, 60

Ravelry, 104–106
Reardon, Megan, 9, 163
receipts, 56
recordkeeping, 42–43,
56–69
references
and retail stores, 198–99
reputation, 46–47
resale certificate, 62
research
about craft fairs, 147–49
resources, 211–14
restocking fee, 197
retail price, 48–51

retail stores, 191–99
  approaching, 194
  and references, 198–99
  and return policies, 197
  selling to, 195–96
return policies, 173–74,
  183–86, 197
Risley, Megan, 9, 136, 177
RSS feed, 91
Ryan, Jenny, 7, 200–201

Sales, 52–53
sales tax, 61–62, 159
Sampler, The, 190
samples, 121, 190, 193–94
schedule
  work, 106
seasonal items, 53
SEO, 91
shipping, 181–82
shops
  brick-and-mortar,
    191–99
  online, 171–90
Sister Diane, 142–44
size
  descriptions of, 176–77
Skelley, Jen, 6
Smith, Liz, 8, 78, 88, 132,
  178, 209–10
social media, 131–41,
  188–89
sole proprietor, 38–39
spam, 112
sponsors
  and podcasting, 109, 143
Squam Art Workshops, 26
staff, 53

stamps
  business name, 68–69
statistics, 91
Stinchcomb, Matt, 9, 28, 67
stores
  brick-and-mortar,
    191–99
  evaluating, 192
  online, 171–90
  owners of, 195–96
stories
  personal, 94, 162
street teams, 79
style
  and blogs, 88
  and photographs,
    175–77
submission guidelines,
  116–17
supplies
  for craft fairs, 150, 161,
    214
swaps
  community, 79–80
Swiger, Tara, 10, 20, 22, 78,
  93, 102, 131, 134, 210

Tags
  business name, 68–69
  and Facebook, 137
  and Flickr, 140
  and online stores, 177
  and YouTube, 138
taxes
  income, 39, 40–41, 43,
    56–59
  sales, 44, 61–62, 159
teaching, 203

terminology
  blog and website, 91
terms
  financial, 198
trading products, 113–14
trunk shows, 203–204
tutorials, 94
Twitter, 132–36

User name, 135

Value
  determining, 46–47
Vaughan, Nicole, 9, 80, 86,
  210
vendor guidelines, 151–52
video, 137–38
vlog, 138
voice, 88

Walrond, Karen, 7, 73–75
websites, 85, 91
  of Creative Collective,
    211–12
  setup of, 86
  submitting to, 81–83
Werker, Kim, 8, 23, 25, 139
wholesale
  orders, 193–94
  pricing, 49–51
word-of-mouth advertis-
  ing, 113
work schedule, 106
workspace, 16–18

YouTube, 137–38

31901046549095